CAUSE AND EFFECT

VISUALIZING SUSTAINABILITY

gestalten

THE EIGHTH WONDER OF THE WORLD

by STEPHAN BOHLE

At the bottom of our hearts, we have a very distinct sense of the fact that our society, our economy, and our way of life must radically change. We must all change our ways. But this is not happening to the extent and at the rate that it should. Lester Brown of the Worldwatch Institute considers the communications industry to be the only agency possessing the capacity to convey the knowledge necessary for sustainable development to the required extent and in the timeframe we have at our disposal.[1] With CAUSE AND EFFECT — VISUALIZING SUSTAINABILITY, we seek to pursue the question of what communication design can contribute to bringing this change about.

Our interest lies in enterprises that have seriously endeavored to anchor sustainable development in their core business, and in designers who convey the complex issue of sustainability by employing an up-to-date, credible, and moving, visual language. We have noticed that many companies, organizations, and institutions dealing with this topic in an exemplary way are not yet utilizing the potentials of successful sustainability communication to the extent that they could. It is therefore high time for visual narratives to provide answers to questions concerning people today: What is going awry, and why? What will my future look like? What solutions are there, and what can I do?

The problem is largely familiar: Mankind has taken the path of non-sustainable development. The world population, the energy demand and CO_2 emissions are bound to increase. Our behavior is leading the planet to—and partially even beyond—the limits of its carrying capacity. In an attempt to counter this, sustainable development seeks to set high economic, ecological and sociocultural standards that are in line with Earth's natural viability. It pursues an intra- and inter-generational principle of justice.[2] Yet the paradox exists that, although people regard climate change and its impacts as a serious threat, by far not all strength is being used to initiate truly sustainable development. We are faced with the often examined gap between knowledge and action, something clearly revealed in the contradiction between environmental awareness and environmental action: Eighty-nine percent of Europeans view climate change as a serious or very serious problem, but only 21 percent are of the opinion

that they bear personal responsibility. Close to 53 percent of the respondents to an EU survey[3] stated that they had taken some sort of measure against climate change in the previous six months. Only two of the 100 largest corporations in the world have expressly taken up the strategic aim of maintaining the ecosystem. Only a single listed firm includes environmental costs in its balance sheet.[4] In many corporations, the attitude still prevails that natural resources are inexhaustible and that sustainability is merely a niche topic.[5]

The communications and design industry has contributed considerably to the industrial nations having adopted a lifestyle that might ultimately push us into the abyss.[6] In the 1950s, economist and retail analyst Victor Lebow wrote that the buying and use of goods ought to be converted into rituals and that people should seek their ego satisfaction in consumption. The aim should be to keep people buying and factories producing. Things ought to be consumed, discarded, burned up, and replaced at an ever-increasing pace.[7] For decades, and in innumerable sales messages, the advertising industry has underpinned precisely this consumerism. In the 1960s, Vance Packard already called advertisers "merchants of discontent," because they put people under the permanent pressure of being dissatisfied, making them measure their happiness exclusively in terms of material possessions.[8]

Only in recent years has it become more and more evident in science, the economy, and society that we cannot rely solely on technological measures (e.g., efficiency and consistency strategies) to solve these fundamental

problems. The real challenge lies in altering people's behavior patterns. What is required is a cultural transformation that includes altered values, rules, and habits. What we really need is an Eighth Wonder of the World to finally be able to transform our society on a large scale into a sustainable one. Neurobiologist Gerald Hüther from the University of Göttingen has been conducting intensive research on how people can change ossified patterns of behavior and thought, and his optimistic findings suggest that such a change is possible. We can fundamentally alter our behavior. What we need in order to do so, however, are so-called neuroplastic messengers, which are released only when we are emotionally moved by something—only then does this doping for the brain set in.[9] The design and communications industry has seduced people to lead a wasteful lifestyle and created a regularity of "always wanting to have everything." For this reason, it must today utilize its potential to enthuse people for sustainable development and support them in making the necessary changes. That is what we call sustainability communication.

THE DESIGN AND COMMUNICATIONS INDUSTRY MUST TODAY UTILIZE ITS POTENTIAL TO ENTHUSE PEOPLE FOR SUSTAINABLE DEVELOPMENT

There is as yet no binding definition of the term, but Florian Brugger of the Leuphana University of Lueneburg[10] has formulated one, which I would like to cite here in a modified and brief form: Sustainability communication comprises all communicative actions related to social and ecological commitment, and to the interrelations of ecological, social, and economic perspectives, with the aim of driving the economy and society forward in the direction of sustainability. Prosperity entails much more than material possessions. It includes education, health, security, employment, leisure time, and environmental quality.[11] Hence, one of the most important tasks of sustainability communication is to draw people's attention to a new quality of life that can be modeled on the sustainable development of society. The task of designers, photographers, artists, and illustrators, and also decision-makers in companies and organizations, is therefore to draw a positive

SUCCESSFUL SUSTAINABILITY COMMUNICATION SENSITIZES PEOPLE, PUTS ITS FINGER ON PROBLEMS AND CREATES A SENSE OF AWARENESS

and desirable picture of the future, to develop specific and sustainable product and service offers—instead of just arguing with a shaking finger and pointing to hopeless future scenarios.

Data, tables, and diagrams have been pushed around for much too long, and too little attention has been given to depicting contents relevant to sustainability in an interesting, comprehensible, and alluring way. Peter M. Senge, director of the Center for Organizational Learning in Cambridge, states: "Trying to get people committed to a sustainability initiative is a bit like trying to be happy: The harder you try, the less successful you're likely to be."[12] What distinguishes successful sustainability communication is that it sensitizes people, puts its finger on problems, and creates a sense of awareness. It arouses enthusiasm, offers guidance, and motivates people to take action. It addresses specific target groups with the aim of reaching the most various stakeholders. It communicates topics of sustainability, conducts PR and communication for environmental and social activities, disseminates information on the environmental impact and social compatibility of products and services, designs sales promotions and events conveying aspects of sustainability, supports and advances strategic consumption, and activates people for the aims of sustainable development. Successful sustainability communication gives attention to the real-life situations of people so that sustainability does not remain an abstract and empty word, but gains relevance. The focus is on positive topics communicated in a way that presents them as desirable and worthwhile (keyword: quality of life). For all too long, the attempt has been made to sell "climate change," but people haven't bought into it. A London-based agency for sustainability communication puts the issue in a nutshell: "Don't sell the sausage, sell the sizzle."[13]

Many enterprises and organizations are on a very good path. Employing extraordinary pictorial languages, they make us curious about the theme of sustainability and its interrelations. They are now spearheading a new generation of creatives, entrepreneurs, and companies taking up the challenge of triggering a change toward sustainability in society and the economy. Their activities have proven to be quite successful, and this has made them role models. Public institutions and ministries, in contrast, still have a hard time addressing the topic. While providing crucial information, they rarely succeed in communicating relevant information in a fashion that arouses and activates people. Also, many companies could make better use of the potentials arising from well-prepared sustainability communication. There is a lot to catch up on. This publication presents practice-oriented and successful examples that can only be recommended. I cordially encourage all readers to match the works and projects presented here. What Paola Antonelli, curator at MoMA, succinctly formulated in a recent issue of the *New York Times* should be our goal: "Sustainability will become normal, integrated in all the other aspects that make life worth living, like humor, imagination, vision, curiosity, humanity, and love."[14] A lot remains to be done, and time is running short. We need this Eighth Wonder of the World, and we need it now.

ABOUT THE AUTHOR

Stephan Bohle is the founder of futurestrategy, a company developing strategies and communication concepts for supporting and advancing sustainable development in enterprises, organizations, and society. He is also a private lecturer on marketing, sustainability communication, and sustainability management at universities in Berlin and Eberswalde. He is a member of the Gesellschaft für Nachhaltigkeit and was appointed to the advisory council of the Deutsche Umweltstiftung in 2010.

FOOTNOTES

1. See Brown 1998
2. See Rogall
3. See European Commission 2011
4. See Puma AG
5. See TEEB 2010
6. See Weizsäcker 2010
7. See Leonard 2010
8. See Packard 1960
9. See Hüther 2011
10. See Brugger 2008
11. See Schmidt-Bleek 2007
12. See Senge 2010, p. 267
13. See futerra 2009
14. See Antonelli 2012

LIST OF LITERATURE

Antonelli, Paola (2012): States of Design 09 — Green Design, New York: New York Times

Brown, Lestern (1998): Vital Signs, New York: Norton

Brugger, Florian (2008): Unternehmerische Nachhaltigkeitskommunikation, Lüneburg: Leuphana Universität Lüneburg

European Commission (2011): Special Eurobarometer 372 Climate Change, auf: http://ec.europa.eu/public_opinion/archives/eb_special_379_360_en.htm#372 (last accessed on 04/14/2012)

futerra sustainability communications (2009): Sell the sizzle, London: futerra

Hüther, Gerald (2011): Was wir sind und was wir sein könnten, Frankfurt: Fischer Verlag

Leonard, Annie (2010): Story of Stuff, London: Constable&Robinson Ltd

OECD (2012): Environmental Outlook to 2050, OECD Publishing: Paris

Packard, Vance (1960): The Hidden Persuaders, London: Penguin Books, 24

Puma AG (2010): PUMA's Environmental Profit & Loss Account (EPL080212final.pdf), at: http://about.puma.com/sustainability/ (last accessed on 04/15/2012)

Rogall, Holger (2009): Nachhaltige Ökonomie, at: http://www.nachhaltige-oekonomie.de/de/nachhaltige-oekonomie.html (last accessed on 04/15/2012)

Schmidt-Bleek, Friedrich (2007): Nutzen wir die Erde richtig?, Frankfurt: Fischer Verlag

TEEB (2010): The Economics of Ecosystems and Biodiversity for Business and Enterprise (TEEB for Bus Exec English.pdf), at: http://www.teebweb.org/ForBusiness/tabid/1021/language/en-US/Default.aspx (last accessed on 04/15/2012)

Senge, Peter M. (2010): The Necessary Revolution, London, Boston: Nicholas Brealey Publishing

Weizsäcker, Ernst Ulrich von (2010): Faktor Fünf, Munich: Droemer, 11

17, De Designpolitie

20, The Architectural League of New York

39, Mathilde Nivet

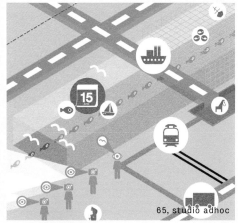

65, studio adhoc

98, Toby Ng Design

118, Infonauts

132, HunterGatherer

145, Nordkapp

161, Amelia Gregory

202, Casanova Pendrill

206, David Rager

220, wurstsack

TABLE OF CONTENTS

CHAPTER 1

ATTENTION IS LUXURY

Each and every day, people deal with more than 10,000 units of information. The consequence is an information overload of around 99 percent, meaning that only 1 percent of the information we take in winds up in our short-term or long-term memory. To "slip into" this 1 percent is one of the three barriers that sustainability communication must overcome. How can it achieve this? First it must invite us to take a look by making use of unusual picture combinations. It must develop a pictorial and formal vocabulary that is extraordinary and sets itself off from everyday monotony.

Sustainability is not perceived as an issue that is really relevant for people. This is the second "hurdle" that has to be overcome. People do not feel personally affected by sustainability. They fail to see the direct connection

react sensitively to changes that take place within a short period of time (heat, coldness, noise, light, weight, pressure, etc.). We barely perceive slow changes. Climate change is not happening "fast enough."[3] That is why we have a very hard time perceiving the long-term nature of problems related to sustainability, which are often characterized by creeping and initially unspectacular processes. Global warming is occurring in millimeter steps, so to speak.[4]

Sustainability communication must therefore succeed in bringing topics of sustainable development to people's minds with a certain degree of consistency. It must try to galvanize us and incite us to think about our future and take action for the sake of our future. Attention is a valuable commodity. In the following chapter, we have compiled works and projects that exemplarily show how provocative, humorous, intelligent, relevant, and eye-catching sustainability communication can and should be.

SUSTAINABILITY COMMUNICATION MUST SUCCEED IN TOUCHING US EMOTIONALLY BY ESTABLISHING A RELATIONSHIP TO OUR EVERYDAY LIFE

between glacier meltdown or the extinction of species and their daily lives. CO_2 is invisible and the factories of low-wage countries are far away. For this reason, Brand calls sustainability a vision without passion that does not have the power to mobilize people by offering the prospect of a better life.[1] Sustainability communication must therefore succeed in touching us emotionally by establishing a relationship to our everyday life. It must seek to translate the highly complex and in part complicated interrelations of sustainability into a comprehensible language.

The third major barrier that successful sustainability communication must overcome is the human psyche. Daniel Gilbert, a professor of psychology at Harvard University, points out that we are descendents of hunters and collectors whose lives were short and whose biggest threat was a man with a stick. This entails that global warming is a threat to our future but not to our next afternoons. We therefore take very little action to avert this alleged threat. "Global warming isn't trying to kill us."[2] Only a small part of our brain is responsible for the future. The largest part is focused on the present. Thus, it takes a lot of time and energy to bring people to deal with questions of the future (see, for example, saving for retirement). Our brain is trained to

FOOTNOTES

1. See Brand 2000
2. See Gilbert 2010
3. See Gilbert ibid.
4. See Brugger 2008

LIST OF LITERATURE

Brand, Karl-Werner (2000): Vision ohne Herzblut. Über die Resonanzfähigkeit des Leitbilds der Nachhaltigkeit, in: politische ökologie 63/64, Vol. 17, 19-22

Brugger, Florian (2008): Unternehmerische Nachhaltigkeitskommunikation, Lüneburg: Leuphana Universität Lüneburg

Gilbert, Daniel (2010): Global Warming and Psychology, in Harvard Thinks Big 2010, www.http://vimeo.com/10324258 (last accessed on 04/23/2012)

Ritchel, Matt: Attached to Technology and Paying a Price. At: New York Times. 06/06/2010 http://www.nytimescom/2010/06/07/technology/07brain.html?_r=1&ref=your_brain_on_computers

Every leaf
traps CO₂.

PLANT
FOR
THE PLANET

Donate trees on
www.plant-for-the-planet.org

Every leaf
traps CO₂.

PLANT
FOR
THE PLANET

Donate trees on
www.plant-for-the-planet.org

LEAVES

by: **Leagas Delaney
Hamburg**

for: **Global Marshall Plan
Initiative, Plant-
for-the-planet.org**

in: **Hamburg, Germany**

Following the goal of planting a billion trees worldwide to get CO_2 emissions levels down, the children's environmental initiative "Plant-for-the-Planet" is always on the lookout to support tree planters. To promote its motto "Stop talking. Start planting.", it initiated a global campaign that takes real leaves both as material, and as a symbol for CO_2 reduction. Inspired by a technique used by Spanish artist Lorenzo Durán, typical climate offenders such as an airplane, a factory, or a car were carved into the leaf green. The resulting quirky visuals compel through simplicity and refreshing straightforwardness. Reproduced as posters and ads, they become clever reminders of the fact that every leaf counts.

WE ONLY USE 10%
OF OUR BRAIN CAPACITY
THANK GOODNESS

10 % — GLACIER, RAINFOREST, FOX

by: JWT Brazil //
Sthefan Ko, Vetor Zero Print,
Lobo
for: Conservation International
in: São Paulo, Brazil

Preserving biodiversity is at the heart of Conservation International's mission. Its 10% campaign aimed to raise public awareness of the impact humans have on environmental conservation. It asks viewers to reconsider their role in climate change and environmental conservation by depicting a rainforest and a glacier carved into pie charts, each with a portion destroyed by human actions. The images draw comparisons between the brain capacity used by humans and the environmental destruction caused by putting that to work. But the message leaves room for hope—there is always the possibility to change our thinking.

LET'S RADICALLY CHANGE OUR THINKING.

THIS HAS BEEN A JEREMYVILLE
COMMUNITY SERVICE ANNOUNCEMENT.

COMMUNITY SERVICE ANNOUNCEMENTS

by: Studio Jeremyville //
    Jeremyville
for: Interface
in: New York, USA

The Jeremyville COMMUNITY SERVICE ANNOUNCEMENTS began in 2010 as a daily, online project. Using simple imagery and words, they aim to connect with people and provide a moment of reflection. Many are focused on the environment, providing tips for consuming less and minimizing waste or pointing out that established ways of thinking could lead to our destruction. They are quiet calls to change both in thought and action.

FIX ME
DON'T DISCARD ME.

THIS HAS BEEN A JEREMYVILLE
COMMUNITY SERVICE ANNOUNCEMENT.

I'M MELTING AWAY.

THIS HAS BEEN A JEREMYVILLE
COMMUNITY SERVICE ANNOUNCEMENT.

LET'S SHED SOME LAYERS.

THIS HAS BEEN A JEREMYVILLE
COMMUNITY SERVICE ANNOUNCEMENT.

WE ARE ALL ON
THIS ISLAND
TOGETHER.
THIS HAS BEEN A JEREMYVILLE
COMMUNITY SERVICE ANNOUNCEMENT.

NATURE

by: Sean Martindale
in: Toronto, Canada

Sean Martindale conducted a thought-provoking experiment: six hand-crafted four-foot-high three-dimensional cardboard letters spelling out the word NATURE on a busy Toronto residential street. Placed alongside regular garbage and recycling bins shortly before sunrise, the lettering did not last for long: Picked up and crushed by one of the city's organic waste and recycling trucks, the cleverly devised installation gained meaning as a thought-provoking impulse. The lack of additional text, explanation or prior notification left residents and passersby wondering.

WWF

THE BIG MELT

iris Amsterdam/GreenGraffiti

Winter was coming to an end, and the ice on the canals in Amsterdam was melting. So with that came an opportunity to remind people about climate change.

The environmentally-friendly QR codes (made from a sheet metal stencil and 'printed' with sticky sand and chalk - it was the first time this technique has been used) were placed on Amsterdam's canals and contained a link to the WWF site which has info on the melting ice caps.

Once temperatures started warming up, the message was clear.

There was no media spend, and there are no laws against printing on ice.

The QR codes were scan-able from the roadside.

They linked to the WWF page on climate change.

THE BIG MELT

by: iris worldwide
(Amsterdam) //
Tom Ormes
for: WWF
in: Amsterdam,
Netherlands

With winter ending and the ice on Amsterdam's canals melting, the World Wildlife Fund took the opportunity to remind people about the effects of climate change on global warming. Using sticky sand and chalk, environmentally friendly QR codes were printed on the canal's ice with sheet-metal stencils. The codes were scannable from the surrounding roads and bridges, linking viewers to a page of the WWF's website about melting polar ice caps. Once temperatures started warming up and the project melted with the ice, the context of the message was made clear.

CONSUME

by: Nicole Dextras
for: grunt gallery
in: Stanley Park,
    Vancouver, Canada

The exhibition "Signs of Change" at the grunt gallery featured the work of Nicole Dextras, who places words sculpted from ice—such as reason, silence, legacy, and desire—into various landscapes. She leaves them to melt, photographing them before they disappear. CONSUME was created as an offsite component for the exhibition and installed at Vancouver's Coal Harbor, where the real estate boom hit hard. The area is located across from Stanley Park, an urban forest with an estimated half million trees, some of which are hundreds of years old. When viewed against the urban backdrop, the melting word suggests the increasing intensity of climate change and makes the viewer wonder how long it will be until the effects of climate change make us disappear too.

GREEN STAMPS

by: De Designpolitie
for: TNT
in: Amsterdam,
    Netherlands

The delivery company TNT commissioned De Designpolitie to design 10 postage stamps for its standard catalog. Designed to bring awareness to environmentally friendly habits everyone can participate in, the 10 stamps are encouraging messages and practical tips for a greener lifestyle, including compensating for carbon emissions, eating organic food, and using green energy.

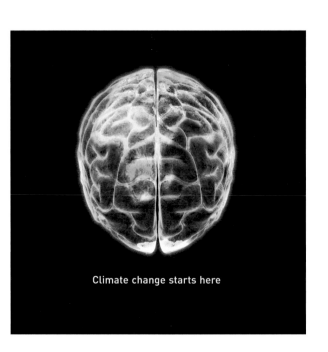

Climate change starts here

CLIMATE CHANGE STARTS HERE

by: imagine' //
    Herman de Jongh
in: Amsterdam, Netherlands

A newspaper ad inspired by an initiative from the ADCN (Art Directors Club Nederland) and the Dutch newspaper *de Volkskrant* that invited participants to share their vision on climate change. Creative director Herman de Jongh led the imagine' team that created the award-winning design, which was published as a full-page ad in *de Volkskrant*.

LIGHT SWITCH STICKER

by: Hu2 Design //
    Antoine Tesquier Tedeschi
in: Paris, France

Turning out the lights—or not turning them on at all—reduces energy bills and is easier on the environment. Hu2 Design's **LIGHT SWITCH STICKERS** playfully remind both adults and kids of the high environmental costs we pay for our energy and that we must use it wisely.

KOMPLOTT— STRESSBLASE 1, TRANKSTELLE

by: salznpfeffer //
    Iven Sohmann, Janina Prenzing
for: University of Applied Sciences Potsdam
in: Potsdam, Germany

The emotionally intelligent signage decals for salznpfeffer's **KOMPLOTT** project serve as friendly reminders in a public restroom that environmentally responsible choices are also important outside of the home. Thought bubbles use a lighthearted tone to remind people to turn off the light, while a decorative decal on the light itself underlines the power needed to keep that light on. A gas tank image over the toilet serves to note that water is not free.

50
IDEAS FOR
THE NEW CITY

#19
USE NATURAL SYSTEMS TO
SUPPORT THE CITY'S INFRASTRUCTURE

The city's wetlands and waterways convey, store, and filter stormwater.
Let's help them do their job.

SEE ALL 50 IDEAS AT URBANOMNIBUS.NET/IDEAS – AND ADD YOURS!

THE ARCHI
TECTURAL
LEAGUE NY

Learn More At
UrbanOmnibus
a project of the Architectural League of New York

FESTIVAL OF
IDEAS FOR
THE NEW CITY
MAY 4–8, 2011

50 IDEAS FOR THE NEW CITY

by: The Architectural League of New York,
Civic Center

for: The Architectural League's Urban Omnibus

in: New York, USA

It was on the occasion of The Festival of Ideas for the New City, a major cultural event co-initiated by the New Museum and a variety of other cultural organizations and institutions, that the Architectural League's Urban Omnibus project developed **50 IDEAS FOR THE NEW CITY**. The selection of particular imaginative concepts and methods to make New York a greener, more livable city has been distilled from features on the Urban Omnibus online publication, a Web platform that encouraged visitors worldwide to add their own ideas to the list. Working with the design studio Civic Center, the Architectural League of New York selected six ideas from the collection to develop a set of posters. Installed on under-utilized surfaces throughout the five boroughs of New York City, the Urban Omnibus project propagates sustainable thinking as fun and essentially creative way of life.

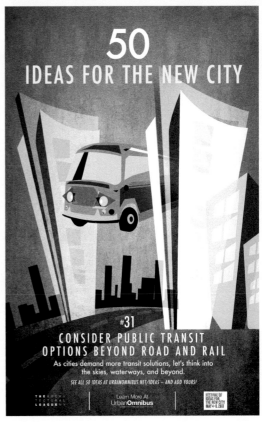

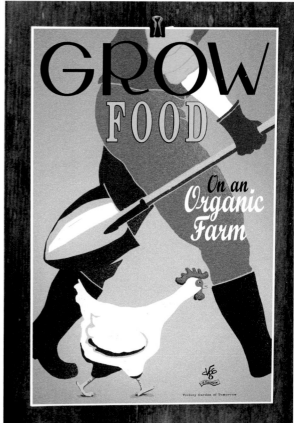

THE VICTORY GARDEN OF TOMORROW

by: J. Wirtheim Communication Design //
    Joe Wirtheim
for: The Victory Garden of Tomorrow
in: Portland (Oregon), USA

Joe Wirtheim's poster campaign THE VICTORY GARDEN OF TOMORROW is inspired by the bold energy of historical propaganda posters. By taking an old form of communication and modernizing it to encourage civic innovation and social action, his posters champion the benefits of eating local food, utilizing empty urban lots and spaces for gardens, and raising chickens. To spread the message even further afield, the illustrations have been made into stickers and T-shirts.

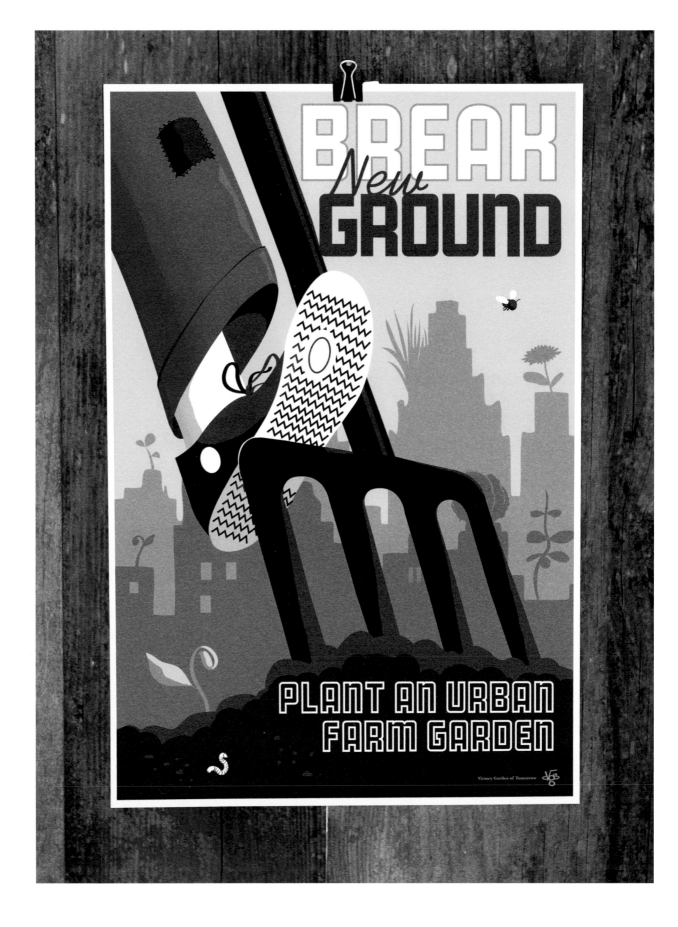

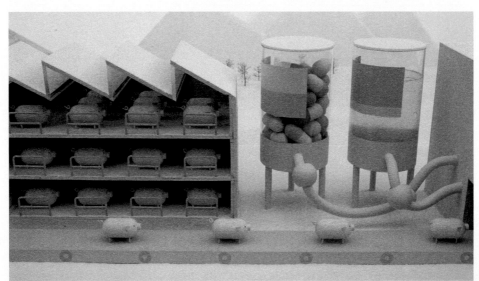

BACK TO THE START

by: Nexus Productions //
    Johnny Kelly
for: Chipotle
in: London, U.K.

The Cultivate Foundation was started by the restaurant chain Chipotle to fund projects that support sustainable agriculture. As part of their education efforts on the environmental benefits of small family farms, they commissioned filmmaker Johnny Kelly to create a short film on the topic. Using stop-motion animation, the film follows a farmer who turns his small farm into an industrial operation. When he realizes that he made the wrong decision, he turns his business back into a more sustainable system.

ROBOTS INSTEAD OF FARMERS

by: Alina Günter

for: W.I.R.E., Abstract Nr.1 2011

in: Zurich, Switzerland

W.I.R.E (Web for Interdisciplinary Research and Expertise) and *Abstract* magazine commissioned Swiss artist Alina Günter to create illustrations for the article "Perspectives on the Rural Future." The article presents four different visions of land use developed using various factors that will determine the future of the countryside. Günter's line drawing is precise but playful, balancing the details of solar panels and wind turbines with shifting perspective.

HELEN / ENERGY EFFICIENCY opposite page

by: Ilja Karsikas
for: Helsingin Energia
in: Finland

An editorial illustration about energy efficiency at home for the Finland-based energy company Helsingin Energia and its customer magazine, *Helen*. The illustration as a whole takes the form of a simple house that contains the interior of a family home as well as the exterior environment. The illustration gently reminds readers that the benefits of making energy-efficient choices extend into the world outside their homes, reinforcing the association of environmentally responsible choices with good feelings.

ECO HOUSE

by: Jan Kallwejt
for: Przekrój Magazine
in: Warsaw, Poland

Jan Kallwejt's illustration for an article about ecological and sustainable building shows the energy-generating possibilities of an eco house. Solar panels on the roof generate electricity for the home's lighting needs and its car battery. A green roof is good for the environment and helps regulate the temperature inside. Thermal energy heats and cools water for washing and heating. Residents benefit from the smart infrastructure of the house, living smartly, comfortably, and responsibly.

CASA INTELIGENTE

by: Comunas Unidas //
    Myrna Cisneros,
    Manuel Córdova
for: Paula Magazine
in: Santiago, Chile

Myrna Cisneros and Manuel Córdova created the illustration CASA INTELIGENTE for an article on smart houses. Their illustration humanizes the house, emphasizing its smart, automatic processes that run the household more efficiently and save energy. It has arms that hold solar panels, operate the security system, water the garden, and help in the kitchen. Faces on the windows and the light color palette reinforce the idea of smart houses as an eco-friendly solution that is also convenient for the homeowner.

WITH THE WAY THE CLIMATE IS CHANGING THE FUTURE LOOKS BLEAK

HOWEVER

MY VISION OF THE FUTURE IS

GREENER TECHNOLOGIES
TO SUSTAIN OUR ENERGY NEEDS

FOR ECO HOMES

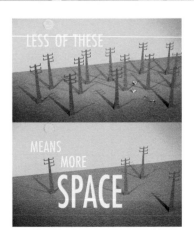

LESS OF THESE

MEANS MORE SPACE

TO PROVIDE CONSISTENT AND SUSTAINABLE CLEAN ENERGY

IDEO'S LIVING CLIMATE CHANGE VIDEO CHALLENGE

by: Freddie Hottinger
for: IDEO
in: U.K.

IDEO'S LIVING CLIMATE CHANGE VIDEO CHALLENGE asked participants to make a video response to global warming that focused on future technologies and presented ideas with a positive and fresh voice. Freddie Hottinger created a stop-motion video that presents future changes to green energy as inevitable and exciting—something that can be looked forward to with anticipation.

HEDONISTIC CONSCIOUSNESS

by: Jan von Holleben
in: Germany

HEDONISTIC CONSCIOUSNESS belongs to the "Homo Ludens 5000" project, a series of photographs developed through playful thinking and collaboration with the goal of promoting sustainable thinking and ideas. The project asks people from various backgrounds to create something that is a cross between photography and their own profession, acknowledging the value of building off of the ideas and expertise of others to create solutions for the future. It is part of photographer Jan von Holleben's larger project, "The Homo Ludens," which is based on understanding the homo ludens, or the man who learns through play.

FORWARD

by: Jan von Holleben

in: Berlin, Germany

In his "Homo Ludens 5000" project, photographer Jan von Holleben celebrates the practice of play for finding creative and practical solutions for environmental problems. Games have become his routine and playing is an essential part of his studio practice. The homo ludens represents the playing human who achieves personal and social development through play. **FORWARD** is an extension of this playfulness, replacing the body of a car with a human body and asking what we have become and what we can change.

RIDE A BIKE ^{opposite page}

by: Riccardo Sabatini

for: Posterheroes

in: Italy

The events organized by Posterheroes encourage debate about environmental issues by giving creatives a platform for their ideas and solutions. Their annual poster challenge asks participants to create a poster based on a chosen theme. Riccardo Sabatini's Posterheroes submission focused on sustainable transportation—the bicycle. His message is simple: using a bicycle for transportation is a win-win situation for the cyclist and the environment.

LOVE YOUR BIKE

by: Creative Concern, Modern Designers

for: Friends of the Earth, Manchester City Council

in: Manchester, U.K.

Creative Concern developed the award-winning **LOVE YOUR BIKE** campaign highlighting personal benefits instead of environmental facts to encourage commuters to get out of their warm, comfortable cars and onto their bikes. A combination of strong visual messages and humor (and a dash of innuendo) communicated the message, which appeared on buses, posters, postcards, online, and at street level, courtesy of volunteers from Friends of the Earth.

SAVE YOUR MONEY.

RIDE A BIKE

IT DOE$N'T NEED FUEL!

AND MAYBE YOU CAN SAVE YOUR ENVIRONMENT TOO!

PRIUS GOES PLURAL CAMPAIGN

by: HunterGatherer,
Saatchi & Saatchi LA
for: Toyota Prius
in: USA

HunterGatherer created an integrated campaign announcing three new models of Toyota's electric hybrid car, the Prius. A series of illustrations and animations were developed for print and online media in which handmade environments were built as landscapes for the new Prius models. These environments, which evoke a healthy natural world, were then used as backgrounds for photographs and stop-animation videos, conveying in a lighthearted way how the choice to drive an electric car is also the right choice for the environment.

EARTHKEEPER PAPER DISPLAY

by: Mathilde Nivet
for: Timberland
in: Paris, France

With her three-dimensional paper landscape, Mathilde Nivet sets a playful yet significant stage for Timberland's new line of organic shoes made of recycled rubber and bio cotton. Portraying the four elements, the display raises the issue of eco-awareness and resourcefulness. A large "Earthkeeper" lettering refers to the brand's tree planting project initiated to accompany the new organic collection. The display was installed at the brand's pop-up store in Paris.

APE ATTACK, KNUT, BAH BAH BLACK SHEEP

by: **NEOZOON**
in: **Paris, France, and Berlin, Germany**

Using discarded fur coats, the street art collective Neozoon creates animal silhouettes on walls and buildings in urban spaces. These street installations remind viewers that the fur coat was a living animal before it became an animal skin with a human inside. The installation of this recycling process in an urban environment references the animals and natural environments that humans continue to destroy.

URBAN JUNGLE ^{opposite page}

by: Ogilvy & Mather Mumbai //
    Mandar Wairkar
for: WWF
in: Mumbai, India

Commissioned to create a WWF campaign that would raise awareness of Mumbai's endangered species, the creatives at Ogilvy & Mather Mumbai focused on the aspects of population growth and urban sprawl. Inspired by the provocative question "Our life at the cost of theirs?" and the traditional folk-art style of Mumbai's state Maharashtra, they developed a series of intricate illustrations. The finished posters merge the familiar silhouettes of a turtle, an elephant, and a rhino with the busy roads, train tracks, and maze of buildings that is the urban jungle.

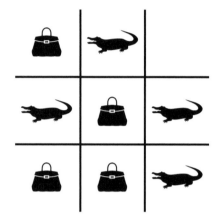

It's your turn.
Visit wwf.sg

NOUGHTS AND CROSSES

by: JWT Singapore
for: WWF
in: Singapore

A large quantity of our planet's species is being exploited for the sake of luxury. Knowing that even well-considered everyday choices can make a big difference, the WWF commissioned JWT Singapore to popularize the issue in a fun and essentially involving way. The result is based on the iconic game of noughts and crosses, prompting people to act, make the right choice, and — eventually — make the winning move.

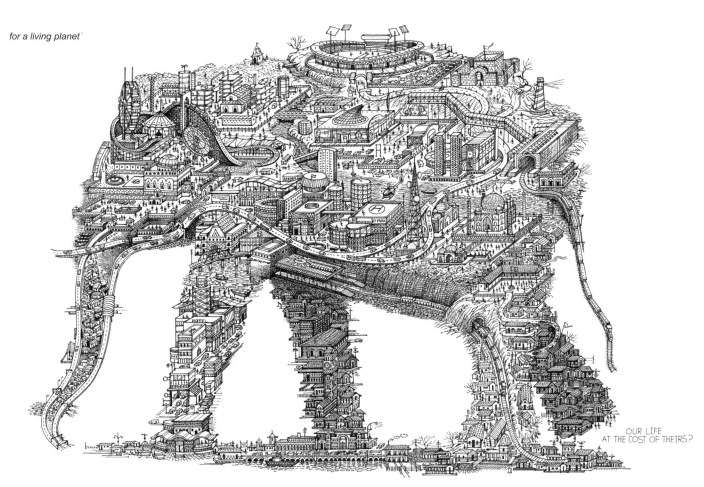

OUR LIFE
AT THE COST OF THEIRS?

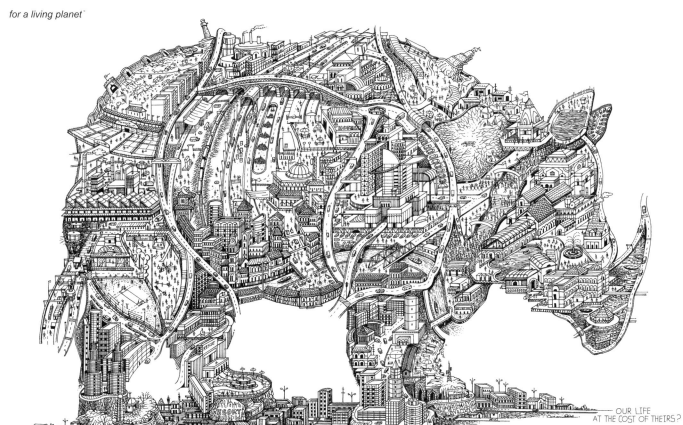

OUR LIFE
AT THE COST OF THEIRS?

Destruction of living spaces cause animal species which provide the continuance of the eco-system to extinct in a faster rate! To bring back the balance, we call for solidarity to protect our own habitat!

DESTRUCTION OF LIVING SPACES

by: Fatih Çevik, Yunus Karaca
for: Gelecek için çeşitlilik platformu
in: Istanbul, Turkey

Designers Fatih Çevik and Yunus Karaca use the traditional Matryoshka doll as a metaphor for the interdependence all species have on each other and the environment. Each doll represents a different animal threatened by extinction—except the smallest one, which features a logger cutting down trees. Destroying natural habitats threatens animals and ultimately humans—to bring the environment back into balance, the piece calls for solidarity in protecting the environment.

REISENDE FRÜCHTE

by: McCann Erickson

for: BUND

in: Germany

BUND's **REISENDE FRÜCHTE** (Fruit Travelers) campaign asks consumers to consider the environmental costs of transporting fruits such as pineapples, bananas, and coconuts by air, water, and truck. For inhabitants of northern climates, buying these fruits has become a habit, as they are so readily available in any location and season. Images of fruits embodying the modes of transportation they are delivered by were printed as posters that could be ordered free of charge from BUND's website. By creating interesting images to be hung at home or in the workplace, the posters serve as a reminder to change habits and choose locally grown produce.

WHALEPOONER, SHARK LOVE

by: Hub Strategy & Communication //
 Jason Rothman, Ben King
for: The Utility Collective
in: San Francisco, USA

Hub Strategy created illustrations printed on plywood—also known as PLYprints—for the Utility Collective. The illustrations were based on Sea Shepherd's worldwide work of defending ocean wildlife. The final images interact with the plywood they are printed on, depicting various scenes such as a whale firing a harpoon from its blowhole and a diver offering a tulip to a shark. By selling ready-to-hang artwork, the project provides financial support to an environmental cause; the prints were sold directly from the Utility Collective's website and traditional retail stores with a portion of each sale donated to the organization and its ongoing missions.

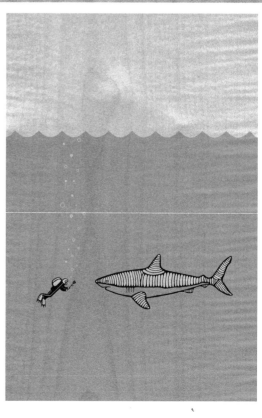

There is a little left.

GREENPEACE
www.greenpeace.ru

WHALE

by: BBDO Moscow //
    Giorgi Popiashvili
for: Greenpeace
in: Moscow, Russia

WHALE was conceived for Greenpeace's print campaign against grey-whale hunting. The bloody close-up of a whale tail poking up through icy waters is accompanied by the small, sparse words, "There is a little left." The message of acting to save the severely threatened gray whale from absolute extinction is communicated by creating a quiet and disturbing image that focuses on the solitary whale to emphasize its dwindling numbers.

GEGEN DEN STROM

by: Leagas Delaney Hamburg

for: Fish & More GmbH // followfish

in: Germany

The dire situation of the world's overfished oceans can still be reversed by sustainable fishing methods, which are practiced by Germany's most sustainable seafood brand, followfish. Using a hand-illustrated animation film, GEGEN DEN STROM (Against the Tide) demonstrates the alarming dimensions of overfished oceans—but with a twist the film makes it clear that there is still hope; by choosing sustainable fish, every consumer can reject industrial fishing and help initiate the change to sustainability.

ES GIBT NICHT VIELE, DIE NOCH

VON HAND FISCHEN.
WIR. UND DER BÄR.

FOLLOWFISH BIETET DEN NACHHALTIGSTEN DOSENTHUNFISCH DER WELT,
DENN ER WIRD EINZELN MIT HANDLEINEN GEFANGEN.

followfish
FOLGE DEM WAHREN GESCHMACK

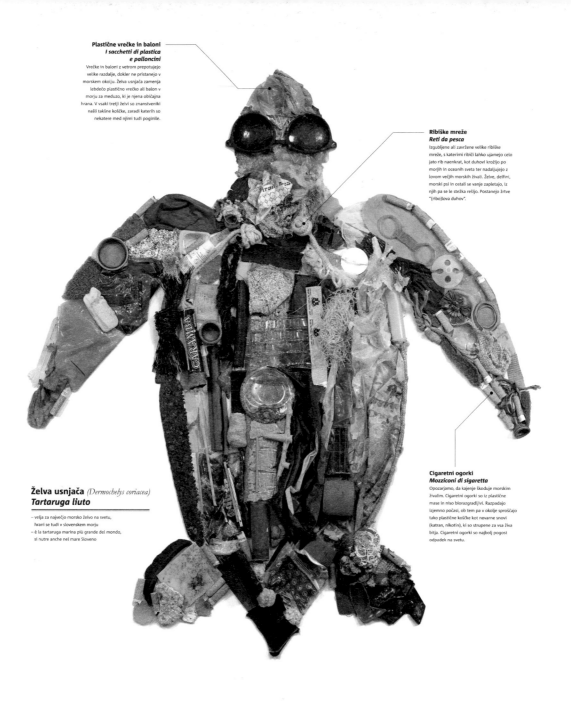

Plastične vrečke in baloni
I sacchetti di plastica e palloncini

Vrečke in baloni z vetrom prepotujejo velike razdalje, dokler se ne pristanejo v morskem okolju. Želva usnjača zamenja lebdečo plastično vrečko ali balon v morju za meduzo, ki je njena običajna hrana. V vsaki tretji želvi so znanstveniki našli takšne koščke, zaradi katerih so nekatere med njimi tudi poginile.

Ribiške mreže
Reti da pesca

Izgubljene ali zavržene velike ribiške mreže, s katerimi ribiči lahko ujamejo celo jato rib naenkrat, kot duhovi krožijo po morjih in oceanih sveta ter nadaljujejo z lovom večjih morskih živali. Želve, delfini, morski psi in ostali se vanje zapletajo, iz njih pa se le stežka rešijo. Postanejo žrtve "(ribo)lova duhov".

Želva usnjača *(Dermochelys coriacea)*
Tartaruga liuto

– velja za največjo morsko želvo na svetu, hrani se tudi v slovenskem morju
– è la tartaruga marina più grande del mondo, si nutre anche del mare Sloveno

Cigaretni ogorki
Mozziconi di sigaretta

Opozarjamo, da kajenje škoduje morskim živalim. Cigaretni ogorki so iz plastične mase in niso biorazgradljivi. Razpadajo izjemno počasi, ob tem pa v okolje sproščajo tako plastične koščke kot nevarne snovi (katran, nikotin), ki so strupene za vsa živa bitja. Cigaretni ogorki so najbolj pogost odpadek na svetu.

MORSKI ODPADNIKI NA SLOVENSKI OBALI
I RINNEGATI MARINI SULLA COSTA SLOVENA

Želvo/galeba/delfina na plakatu smo sestavili iz morskih odpadkov, nabranih na slovenski obali. Odpadki po rekah, s kanalizacijo, z ladij ali s kopnega dosežejo morje, ki jih naplavi na obalo ali pa jih tam odložijo obiskovalci. Smeti vidno onesnažujejo našo obalo, ovirajo plovne poti in ladje, čedalje večja grožnja pa so morskim živalim ter rastlinam. Slovensko obalo že nekaj let vsak mesec v celoti očistimo morskih odpadkov. Le kakšna bi obala bila, če bi odpadke pustili tam? Skupaj moramo rešiti ta problem. Poskrbimo za manj odpadkov in skrbno ravnanje z njimi. Pridružite se mesečnim čiščenjem slovenske obale. Več informacij: www.ecovitae.org.

MARINE RENEGADES OF THE SLOVENIAN COAST

by: Lukatarina
for: Eco Vitae
in: Slovenia

Lukatarina's educational poster series for Eco Vitae draws attention to the littering of the Slovenian coast and its endangered species. Taking flotsome and jetsome found on the beach as material for a series of illustrations, Lukatarina created a bottlenose dolphin, a leatherback sea turtle, and a herring gull that are not yet threatened with extinction, but very typical for the region. The striking motives serve as infographics, offering valuable clues about what kind of objects pose the greatest danger to the depicted animals: fishing nets for the dolphin, pieces of hard plastic for the gull, and plastic bags for the turtle. The title **MARINE RENEGADES** creates significant verbal ambiguity, as the Slovenian word for renegade has the same word stem as that for waste or litter.

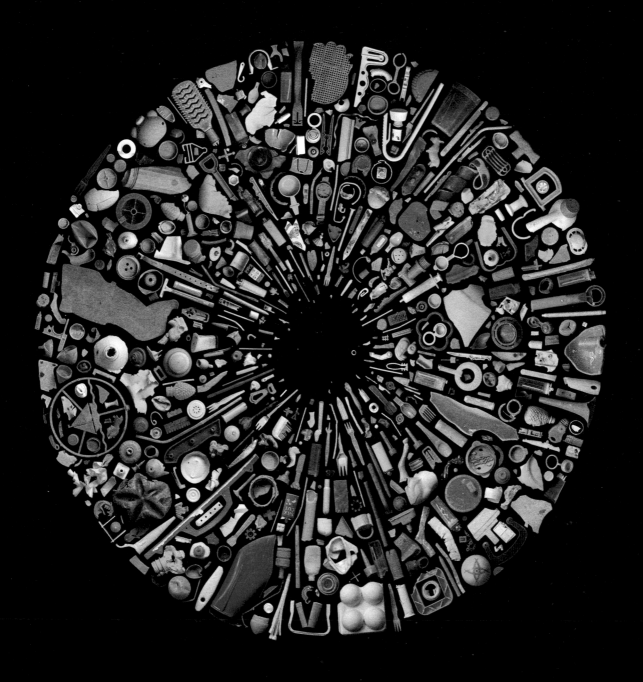

SOUP: 500+

by: Mandy Barker
in: Leeds, U.K.

Soup is the term for plastic garbage floating in the sea. This series aims to evoke an emotional response in the viewer by combining a contradiction between initial aesthetic attraction and an awareness of the disturbing volume of these plastics, which have no boundaries and result in the deaths of sea creatures. All of the plastics in the work were salvaged from beaches around the world. SOUP: 500+ represents more than 500 pieces of plastic debris found in the digestive tract of a dead albatross chick in the North Pacific Gyre.

PLASTIC IS NOT FANTASTIC

by: Tatiana Woolrych

in: London, U.K.

The photo for Tatiana Woolrych's infographic, **PLASTIC IS NOT FANTASTIC**, is made from one month's plastic usage in a London household of five. Underneath the photo, each of the seven recyclable plastics are listed, including the amount of time they need to biodegrade and what their most common uses are. But the real message is that four out of the seven are often not recycled at all due to the mixture of compounds they are made from. Instead of just delivering the message that plastic is bad, the project gives viewers sinformation that is easy to remember so that they can be more aware of the plastics they buy and know what to avoid.

BAGFOOT opposite page

by: Lukatarina

in: Slovenia

Lukatarina's Bag on Bag "trash art" awareness campaign is spun around the odd-looking creature **BAGFOOT**. Asserting to have run into the member of a new hominid species on their sunday walk somewhere near Ljubljana, Lukatarina spread the message on YouTube and Facebook, and as unexpected interventions on the streets of Ljubljana, on local TV shows, on the morning and evening news, on public transport displays, and in newspaper articles. Posing the question of whether **BAGFOOT** is a new hominid species, or just some sort of a virus, a clever hoax up for everyone's guess, the campaign addresses the devastating effects of litter pollution in a way that is just as much fun as it is thought-provoking.

PLASTIC IS NOT FANTASTIC

POLYETHYLENE TEREPHTHALATE (PET, PETE)	HIGH DENSITY POLYETHYLENE (HDPE)	POLYVINYL CHLORIDE (PVC, VINYL)	LOW DENSITY POLYETHYLENE (LDPE)	POLYPROPYLENE (PP)	POLYSTYRENE (PS)	OTHER (O)
300–1,000 years in a landfill or 10 to 20 years if exposed to the elements.	Depending on the thickness of the plastic it could take up to 100 years.	Does not really degrade and when it does it gives off a number of toxic chemicals.	500 to 1000 years. If there is no exposure to light, for example in a landfill, the plastic can remain intact indefinitely.	This material is highly resistant to photo degradation and will not decay for millennia.	No known microorganism can biodegrade it. If left exposed to sunlight it will achieve photo degration and break-up within 50 years.	This type of plastic is made from a mixture of any of the previous types. It does not break down easily, if at all, and is considered permanently chemically bonded.
DRINK BOTTLES, VACUUM FORMED PACKAGING, SWEETS AND CRISP BAGS, FOOD CONTAINERS, OVENIBLE AND MICROWAVABLE FOOD TRAYS...	DETERGENT BOTTLES, BLEACH BOTTLES, MILK CARTONS, SHAMPOO/CONDITIONER BOTTLES, CEREAL BOX LINER...	VARIOUS VACUUM FORMED PACKAGING, PIPES, WINDOW FRAMES, CHILDRENS TOYS...	PLASTIC BAGS, SHRINK WRAP AND STRETCH FILM, COATINGS FOR PAPER CARTONS, SQUEEZABLE BOTTLES...	BOTTLE TOPS, YOGURT, MARGARINE AND FOOD CONTAINERS, ROPE, MEDICINE BOTTLES, CLOTHING, YOGURT POTS...	STYROFOAM PACKAGING PEANUTS, CUPS, PLATES, MEAT AND POULTRY TRAYS, BOWLS, CUTLERY...	BOTTLES, PLASTIC LUMBER APPLICATIONS, SAFETY SHIELDS AND GLASSES...

TYPES 4 TO 7 PLASTICS ARE RARLY RECYCLED DUE TO THE MIXTURE OF COMPOUNDS THAT THEY ARE MADE FROM

**Älska
återanvändning**

Bra för dig. Bra för dem som har det svårt. Och bra för miljön.

MYRORNA

ÄLSKA ÅTERANVÄNDNING

WE LOVE REUSAGE

by: Ruth Stockholm //
   Kari Modén, Jenny Berg, Anders Granberg
for: Myrorna, Sweden's largest chain of second-
   hand stores.
in: Stockholm, Sweden

The Swedish second-hand store Myrorna is
a part of the Salvation Army. They believe in
recycling clothing, furniture, toys, and other
household goods not only because it is good
for the environment, but because the surplus
goes to helping people in need. Myrorna commissioned advertising agency Ruth to create a
fresh version of the recycling symbol for use
in their stores, in their advertising materials,
and on their website. The result is a recycling
symbol turned into a heart that emphasizes
the most important goal of donating—helping
others and the environment.

TIDYMAN COLLECTION ^{opposite page}

by: My Poor Brain //
   Tim Smith
in: London, U.K.

The **TIDYMAN COLLECTION** documents the countless ver-
sions of the Tidyman—the iconic stick figure on packaging
and signs who demonstrates to all consumers how to put litter into the trash bin. Tim Smith's ongoing collection is a look
at the versatility of the widely used image, which has been
adapted and personalized to communicate an instructive
message in a humorous way.

Stop hiding problems.
Let's start by participating the 25, 26 and 27 of September in **Puliamo il Mondo.**

live sustainably.

Puliamo il Mondo
LEGAMBIENTE

PULIAMO IL MONDO

by: Forchets //
Livio Grossi
for: Legambiente
in: Milan, Italy

Part of an initiative called "Clean Up the World" that Legambiente participates in every year, Forchets's **PULIAMO IL MONDO** campaign focuses on the problem that many serious environmental issues are swept under the carpet instead of being addressed and dealt with sufficiently. Taking the problem literally and with a touch of sarcasm, Livio Grossi and his team set up a series of carpet-sweeper scenes at famous public places in Milan.

WHEN
WE POLLUTE
THE SEA,
WE POLLUTE FOR
A LONG TIME.

Surfrider
Foundation
E U R O P E

HELP US
KEEP THE OCEAN
CLEAN

FOSSILS opposite page

by: Young & Rubican Paris
for: Surfrider Foundation
in: Europe

"When we pollute the sea, we pollute for a long time." Seeking to visualize the problem and engage people to keep the ocean clean, the Surfrider Foundation, in collaboration with the Marine Litter program, commissioned Young & Rubican, Paris, who came up with a series of striking visuals. Plastic bottles and tins, fossilized among ammonites, serve as alarming reminders of the fact that throwing things into the ocean will impact the Earth in the very long run.

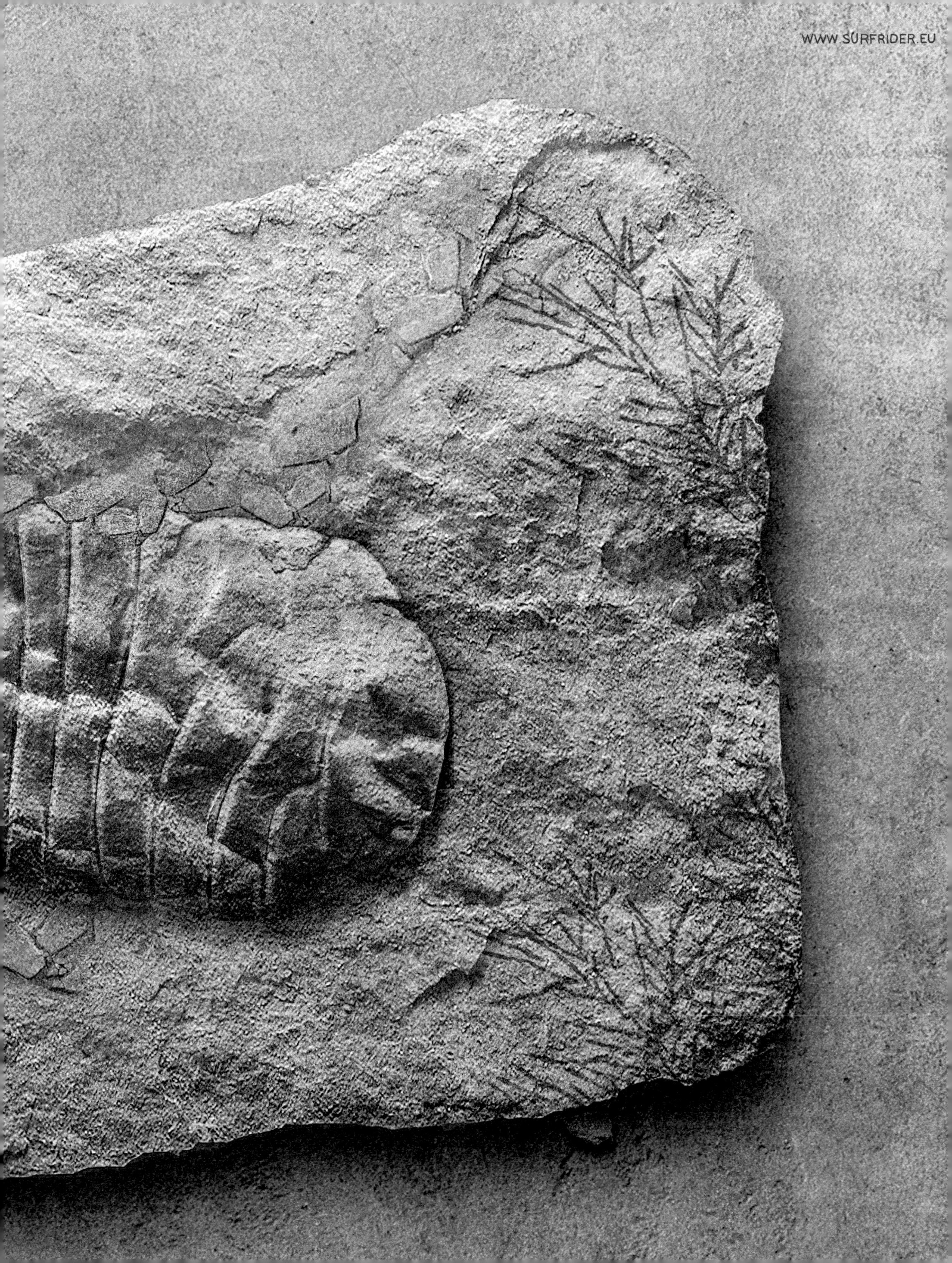
WWW.SURFRIDER.EU

Volg je Hart

Gebruik je Hoofd

Volg je Hart
Gebruik je Hoofd

Triodos ✿ Bank

FOLLOW YOUR HEART — USE YOUR HEAD

by: Dawn //
 Christian Borstlap
for: Triodos Bank
in: Netherlands

According to the *Financial Times*, Triodos is the most sustainable bank in the world—and the most unknown. As an introduction to a wider audience that would appreciate its commitment to environmental, social, and cultural organizations, Dawn translated the company's philosophy into a major campaign: "Follow your Heart, Use your Head." These two seemingly contradictory terms are successfully united in the colorful character of the campaign, which represents the bank's willingness to do business on its own terms and sets it apart from other financial institutions.

OCCUPY GEORGE

by: Occupy George //
Andy Dao, Ivan Cash
in: San Francisco, USA

OCCUPY GEORGE circulates dollar bills stamped with fact-based infographics, informing the public of America's daunting economic disparity one bill at a time. For those who want to join the project, the group's website offers a downloadable template with instructions for printing on the bills at home. By moving the Occupy Wall Street protest to American currency, OCCUPY GEORGE spreads the message to a wider audience.

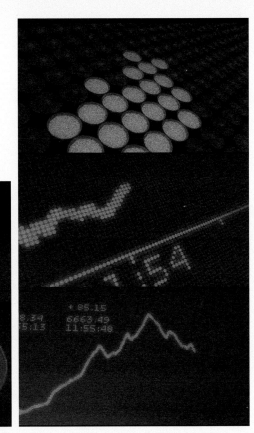

by: 10hoch16
for: Oxfam
in: Berlin, Germany

This one-minute advertising spot was produced for Oxfam's campaign against food speculation. A bowl of food surrounded by the quiet noises of a home becomes one of many dots on a commodities trading board and from there changes into a heart monitor in a hospital that quickly falls quiet. The message that speculation on food commodities results in starvation and death is conveyed quickly and powerfully.

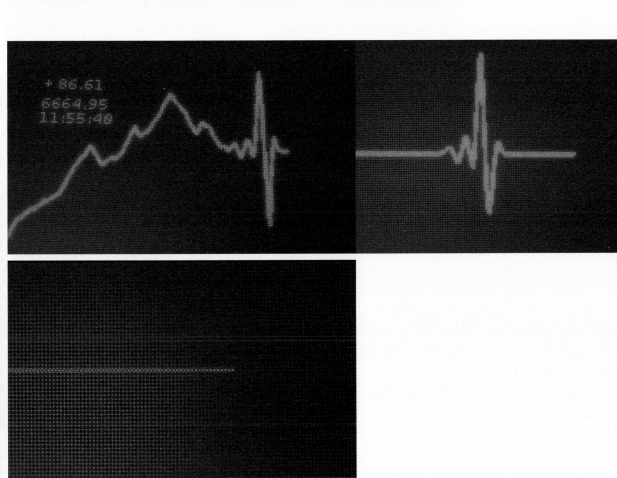

CHAPTER 2

FOR THEY KNOW NOT WHAT THEY CAN DO

We know that people who feel they are informed about climate change (its causes and consequences, and possibilities to take action against it) are more likely to take measures to actively fight against it than those who feel poorly informed.[1] In a survey requested by the European Commission,[2] 34 percent of European citizens said that they would like to do something to combat climate change

The dry listing of facts and pie charts are not a big help. In the past years, we have witnessed a remarkable development in the field of so-called infographics. They are visually highly attractive, develop their own unusual picture and sign languages, and draw the viewer into the respective subject. In the following chapter, we present infographics and illustrations that show interrelations in an exciting and entertaining fashion, provide background information, inform the public, and create a true awareness and understanding of themes related to sustainability.

INFORMATION ON THE TOPICS OF SUSTAINABLE DEVELOPMENT MUST BE PREPARED IN SUCH A WAY THAT LOOKS INVITING AND MAKES PEOPLE CURIOUS

but did not know what. Around one-fourth (26 percent) of the respondents were of the opinion that it would have no effect on climate change if they altered their behavior, and 15 percent were convinced that it would be too expensive to do something against climate change. In the United States 65 percent believe that climate change is not a serious problem; they ignore the topic or mistake climate change for the hole in the ozone layer.[3] So if information is a crucial precondition for taking sustainable action, sustainability communication bears a special responsibility. Information on the topics of sustainable development must be prepared in such a way that it looks inviting and makes people curious.

FOOTNOTES

1. See Eurobarometer ibid.
2. See Eurobarometer 2008
3. See Lloyd 2011

LIST OF LITERATURE

European Commission 2011: Eurobarometer Climate Change, at: http://ec.europa.eu/public_opinion/archives/eb_special_379_360_en.htm#372 (last accessed on 04/24/2012)

Lloyd, Robin (2011): Why Are Americans So Ill-Informed about Climate Change?, at http://www.scientificamerican.com/article.cfm?id=why-are-americans-so-ill (last accessed on 04/24/2012)

The Baltic Sea region – a dynamic picture

Transnational Connectivity

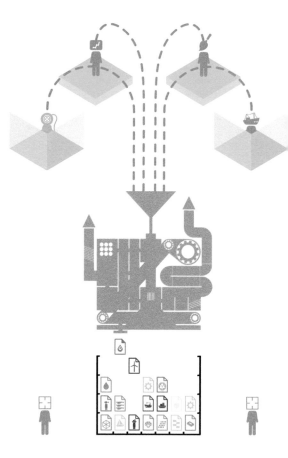

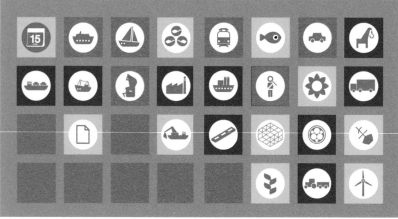

BALTSEAPLAN VISION 2030 — TOWARDS THE SUSTAINABLE PLANNING OF BALTIC SEA SPACE

by: studio adhoc
for: s.Pro — sustainable projects, German Federal Maritime and Hydrographic Agency
in: Baltic Sea Space

The EU project **BALTSEAPLAN** addresses sustainable maritime planning. It considers natural conditions as well as current uses and conflicts when writing proposals for cross-national maritime strategy. Studio adhoc developed the visual identity for the project and online communication tools that allow partners from different countries to work together and share their experiences. The complex content was communicated with a brochure available in English, Estonian, and Lithuanian and a comprehensive icon language that was designed to represent sophisticated topics in transportation, fishing, and industry in a pleasant and understandable way.

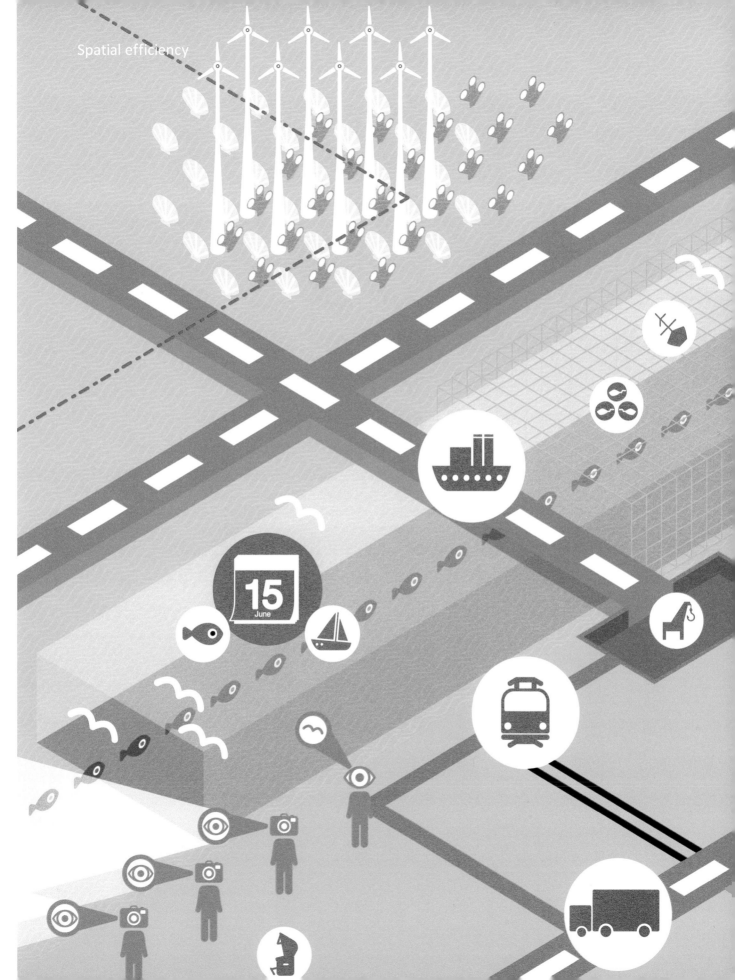

Spatial efficiency

-09 in Kollektorfläche

△52,53%

2005:	2006:	2007:	2008:	2009:
233.500 m²	292.700 m²	281.019 m²	347.720 m²	356.170 m²
	△25,35%	▽4,04%	△23,74%	△2,43%

Austria Solar Jahresbericht 2011   Quelle: BMVIT/Biermayr 2010   23

THE AUSTRIA SOLAR ANNUAL REPORT

by: Serviceplan
for: Austria Solar
in: Austria

Solar energy is Austria Solar's business. Serviceplan used a new printing technology to create a sun-driven annual report in which the information in the report only became visible when sunlight hit the pages. The project represented the importance of sunlight in a simple yet playful manner and how sunlight can be converted into other forms of energy. This unusual presentation reflected Austria Solar's business and its values as a consistently innovative organization for the Austrian solar sector.

(5) ▬▬▬ BRAZIL 298
(4) ▬▬▬ MEXICO 323
(3) ▬▬▬▬ CHINA 691
(2) ▬▬▬▬▬▬ INDIA 1139
(1) ▬▬▬▬▬▬▬ USA 1500

TOP 5 NEED IN MILLION CUBIC METERS OF WATER

DOMESTIC WATER USE
URBAN AREAS WILL INCREA
AS A RESULT OF POPULATI
GROWTH AND URBANISATI

THIS WILL REQUIRE NEW WAT
INFRASTRUCTURE IN MA
COUNTR

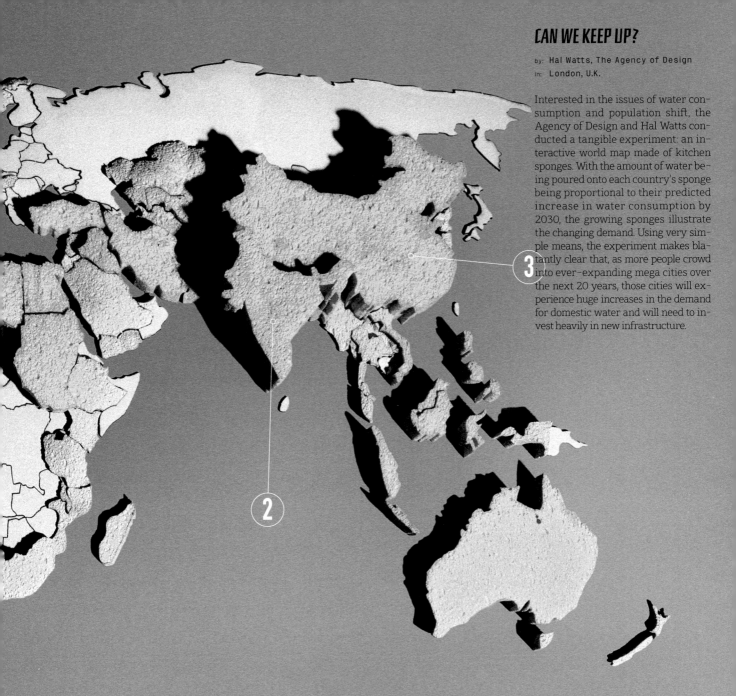

CAN WE KEEP UP?

by: Hal Watts, The Agency of Design
in: London, U.K.

Interested in the issues of water consumption and population shift, the Agency of Design and Hal Watts conducted a tangible experiment: an interactive world map made of kitchen sponges. With the amount of water being poured onto each country's sponge being proportional to their predicted increase in water consumption by 2030, the growing sponges illustrate the changing demand. Using very simple means, the experiment makes blatantly clear that, as more people crowd into ever-expanding mega cities over the next 20 years, those cities will experience huge increases in the demand for domestic water and will need to invest heavily in new infrastructure.

CAN WE KEEP UP?

CREASE IN URBAN DOMESTIC WATER USE BY 2030

BOTTLED WASTE

by: Hal Watts
in: London, U.K.

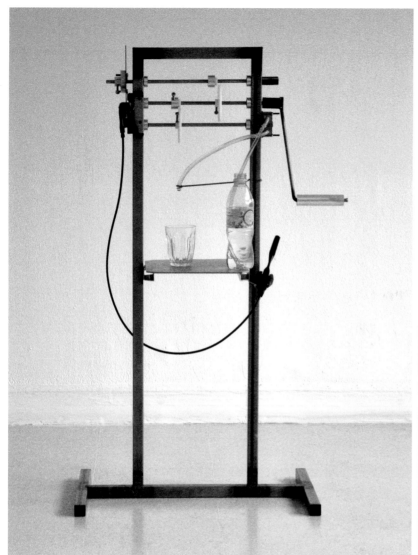

BOTTLED WASTE is an installation that looks into the impact of bottle water. The fact that a liter of bottled water embodies more than 1000 times more energy than a bottle of tap water is hard to imagine, let alone visualize. Understanding that an image will only convey the problem to a certain level, Hal Watts decided to render the issue tangible by means of an interactive installation that would make people learn the hard way: Amid a smart set-up of gearings, a small pump, and a brake, the user must turn the pump handle for approximately three hours to pump one liter of water, making up for the amount of energy embodied in the bottled water. By moving a clutch the pump can be set to tap water, in which case it pumps faster and the brake is disengaged, meaning that the user can pump a liter in under 20 minutes, using 1000 times less energy.

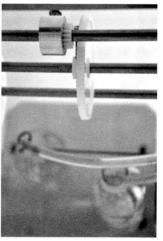

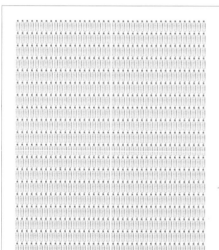

BOTTLED WATER USES
1000 TIMES MORE ENERGY
THAN **TAP WATER**.

ENERGY BEHAVIOURS ^{opposite page}

by: Native Design, The Agency of Design //
    Rich Gilbert, Matthew Laws, Adam Paterson
for: Moixa Energy
in: London, U.K.

Energy conservation on an industrial scale can lead to large savings — especially where high-intensity manufacturing processes are involved. "Can We Stop The Energy Leak" is a visualization of energy use. Installed as a focal point for workers in a large factory, it drops metal balls into metal buckets from three hoppers that represent three different parts of the factory. Driven by live factory energy data, each ball dropped represents 0.5 kilowatts of energy. As the minutes, hours, and days pass, it becomes clear which areas of the factory are using the most energy. The hoppers can be compared side by side, encouraging competition between different departments to conserve more energy.

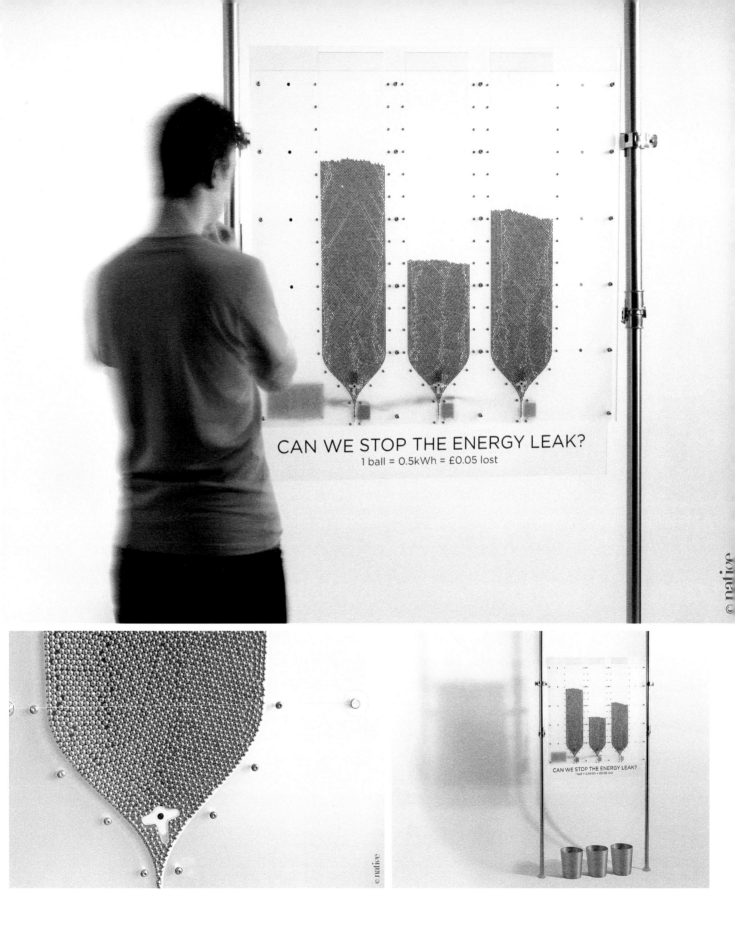

CAN WE STOP THE ENERGY LEAK?

1 ball = 0.5kWh = £0.05 lost

© native

© native

THE CLIMATE MACHINE

by: The Agency of Design //
     Matthew Laws

for: Royal College of Art
     graduation project

in: London, U.K.

If the United Kingdom wants to meet environmental goals to stop global warming by the year 2050, it will have to reduce its carbon footprint by 90 percent. THE CLIMATE MACHINE invites users to discover their own contribution to the problem by entering their daily habits into an iPad, which evaluates and displays their energy and carbon footprints. It uses a mirror and light bulbs as indicators of large or small footprints. The mirror, which changes in clarity based on the user's carbon footprint, is surrounded with 200 light bulbs that switch on and off to represent their energy footprint. On the back is a more detailed visualization of the energy and carbon data, which visitors can use as a starting point for consumption changes.

Carbon notice

WARNING!
Amount of carbon in the atmosphere at extreme levels.

You've added all 8 human sources of carbon. Human activities are emitting carbon into the atmosphere. Being taken out by natural processes.

Press the blue button to continue

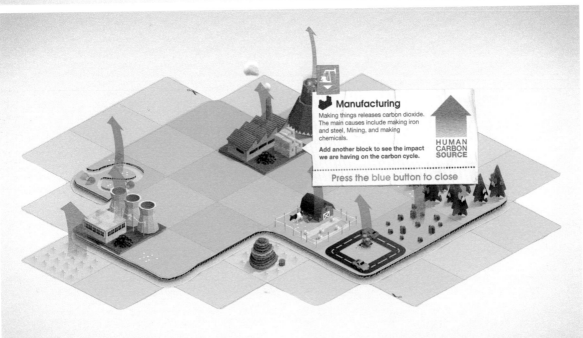

Manufacturing

Making things releases carbon dioxide. The main causes include making iron and steel, Mining, and making chemicals.

Add another block to see the impact we are having on the carbon cycle.

HUMAN CARBON SOURCE

Press the blue button to close

Welcome to Carbon cycle

Press the blue button to start

Carbon notice

Be careful...
The amount of carbon in the atmosphere is increasing,

You've added 1 human source of carbon.

Human activities are emitting carbon into the atmosphere. More carbon is now being released than is being taken out by natural processes. This increases the amount of carbon in the atmosphere.

Press the blue button to continue

CARBON CYCLE

by: GR/DD //
Tim Smith
for: The Science Museum
in: London, U.K.

The climate science gallery at London's Science Museum is dedicated to teaching museum visitors about the science behind climate change. The museum commissioned GR/DD to develop an interactive game that clarifies the complex subject of the carbon cycle and demonstrates how it can be manipulated in a positive way. Players add various natural or man-made elements to the digital island by placing blocks on a physical grid. As users try to balance the amount of carbon in the atmosphere by adding and removing blocks, they receive relevant information about the science behind the cycle.

COUNTING CARBON

by: Native Design, The Agency of Design //
    Rich Gilbert, Matthew Laws, Adam Paterson
for: London Transport Museum
in: London, U.K.

Carbon dioxide is often described in terms of grams, a measurement that is hard to visualize and commonly misunderstood. In this installation, giant balloons are inflated with the amount of carbon dioxide released by a range of everyday activities and products. The exhibit makes the numbers surrounding climate change more relatable, leaving a lasting impression on viewers that could never be achieved only with numbers. Produced at Native Design for the "Sense and the City" exhibition at the London Transport Museum.

AMAZON
BASIN
-23 MM ▼

SEASONAL AND
LONGTERM CHANGES
IN GROUNDWATER LEVELS
HEADSUP2012.COM

SPRING
2009

○ GROUNDWATER
DEPLETION

SAHARA AQUIFER ▼   SAUDI ARABIA ▼   NORTH CHINA PLAIN ▼   NORTHERN INDIA ▼

SOURCES: NASA GRACE Satellite Data JC Center for Hydrologic Modeling, Decadal Groundwater Depletion USGS

SEASONAL AND LONG-TERM CHANGES IN GROUNDWATER LEVELS

by: Studio Richard Vijgen //
Richard Vijgen

for: HeadsUP!, Peggy Weil

in: New York, USA

In March of 2002 NASA launched the so-called GRACE mission, which consists of two satellites designed to measure and map the Earth's gravity fields. Each month the two satellites complete a full scan of the Earth, allowing scientists to study how variations in the Earth's gravity fields — from which changes in groundwater levels can be derived — are developing over time. With SEASONAL AND LONG-TERM CHANGES IN GROUNDWATER LEVELS, Studio Richard Vijgen developed an interactive data visualization that uses the measurements collected by the GRACE satellites over a period of 10 years to illustrate seasonal and long-term changes in groundwater levels compressed to a 30-second animation. The 19,000-square-feet Nasdaq screen on Times Square shows a map of the world through the eyes of GRACE, a topography made of measurement data. It shows the yearly cycle of groundwater depletion and replenishment, the rainy seasons in the Amazon, and parts of the world suffering from yearly droughts. Visualized on a global scale for the first time, the measurements reveal that some areas show a steady decline in groundwater levels. Displayed as a virtual gauging rod on the high screen of the Reuters building, these long-term changes throw light on the necessity to use groundwater responsibly. The impressive scale and technological intricacy of the installation reflect the beauty and overwhelming complexity of the natural cycle, while rendering it a spectacular show to appeal to the masses passing by. An interactive feature allows the audience to engage with the visualization by adding their own city to be displayed on a scrolling ticker of worldwide historical groundwater levels using a mobile application. An accompanying website keeps an archive of over 600 cities that have been submitted.

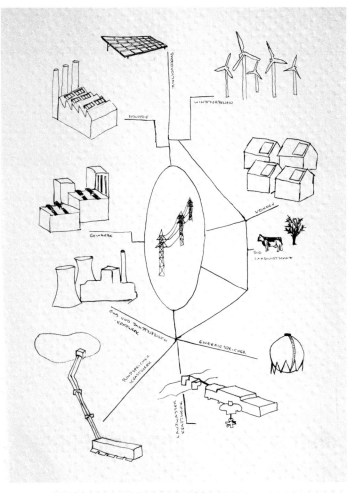

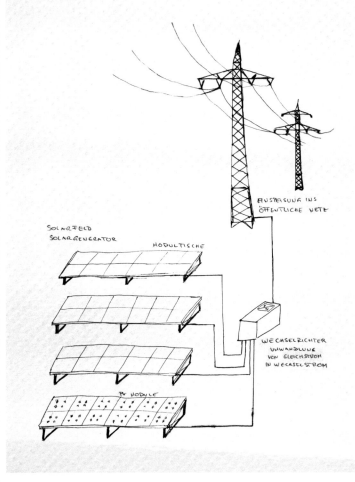

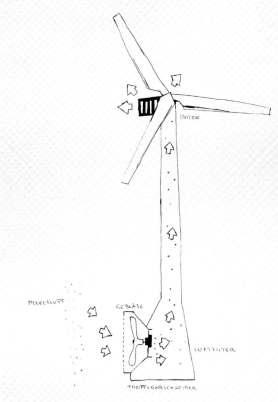

GENERATING RENEWABLE ENERGY

by: Esther Gebauer
for: Stern
in: Germany

A group of illustrations for an article in the popular German magazine *Stern* about engineers inventing new ways of generating energy from renewable sources. The sketchy images appear to have been drawn on napkins, reinforcing the idea of using creative thinking to find solutions for sustainable energy.

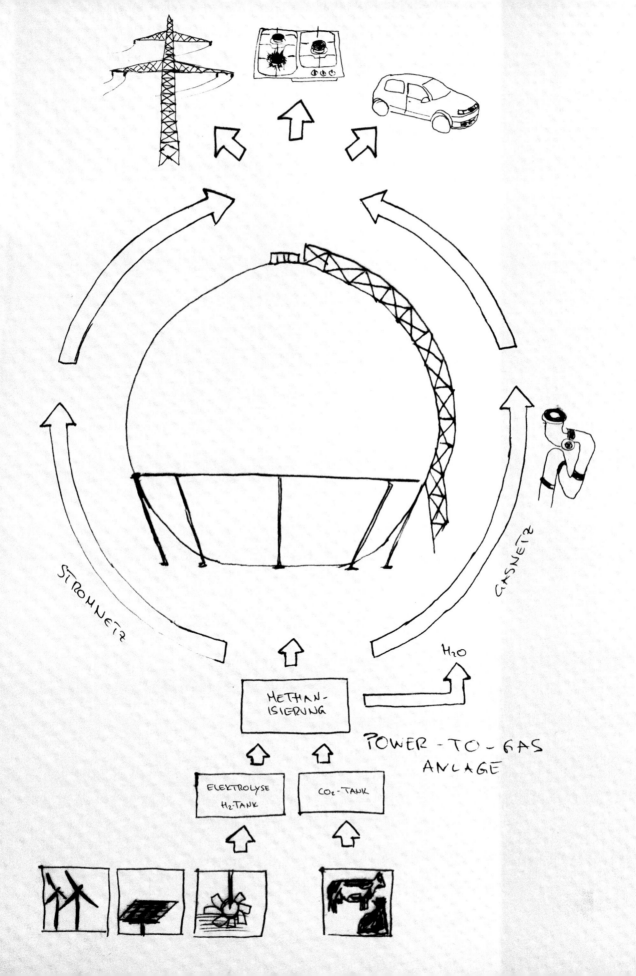

STROMNETZ

GASNETZ

H_2O

METHAN-
ISIERUNG

POWER-TO-GAS
ANLAGE

ELEKTROLYSE
H_2-TANK

CO_2-TANK

An Introduction to Lighting

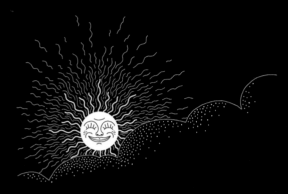

FUN FACT 1:

Most Infrared rays from the sun are blocked by ordinary window glass. A sunny room warms up because objects in the room absorb the sun's visible light and convert it to infrared, which can't get out through the windows.

One of the oldest proclamations in Western literature—maybe the very oldest, depending on how you see things—is "Let there be light." And for most of human history, whether we dwelled in caves or in Gilded Age mansions, light was inseparable from heat: Domestic lighting consisted of either letting sunlight inside or burning something organic. The Egyptians were making candles from beeswax and animal fat 5,000 years ago, and except for the discovery of new fuel sources—whale oil, ahoy!—the candle continued to illuminate homes deep into the 19th century.

Windows, until the development of cheap and effective glass manufacturing, were originally small things that weren't much more than holes in the wall. Their usefulness had to be balanced between the amount of light they let in and the amount of heat and smoke they let out. Yet in situations where money was no object, as in the construction of the great European cathedrals, windows could be used for illumination far more effectively (and beautifully) than any other form of light. As the technology developed, the construction of the window-rich stately old homes of England (particularly Hardwick Hall, "More glass than wall") in the 1590s set architects on the path of bringing more sunlight into everyone's home.

The widespread development of natural gas lighting around the 1820s, followed 60 years later by the gas mantle (a piece of radioactive thorium that glowed brighter than a gas flame when heated by

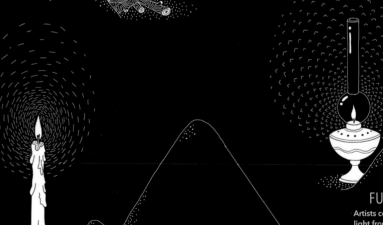

Story by TK
Photos by TK

FUN FACT 2:

Artists commonly prefer the light from windows facing the nearest pole (north light, in the northern hemisphere), since that light varies the least as the sun moves throughout the day.

Dwell

re the last hurrah of the large scale
's to produce light. To the jeers of
as lamps everywhere, in the 1880s in-
ent electric.

dison's invention still didn't separate
The incandescent lamp worked by
'nt of electricity through a thin tungsten
'ved. The bulb gave off light, but only
of the enormous amounts of heat cre-
, incandescent lamps convert, at best,
of their energy to visible light. The sale
ghts in the 1930s brought a slightly
of producing light, but it has only
vely recently that cold light has moved
the home.

the midst of a revolution in interior
'chnologies to produce light are being
—at least in America, where lighting
proximately 9 percent of America's
hey all may soon be regulated by the
Energy and Security Act of 2009.
hat bill is dedicated to lighting stan-
for all electric lights manufactured
utput at least 80 lumens per watt of
ficiency of about many times greater
andescent light bulbs! But that's only
. For the foreseeable future our hous-
by a variety of means, including high-
direct or indirect sunlight, and, from

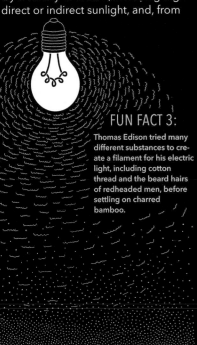

FUN FACT 3:

Thomas Edison tried many
different substances to create a filament for his electric
light, including cotton
thread and the beard hairs
of redheaded men, before
settling on charred
bamboo.

Words You Should Know

Incandescence: The light given off
when an object is heated. As the heat
increases, the color of the light mimics
the spectrum: Cooler objects glow
reddish-orange, hotter objects glow
yellow, very hot objects glow bluish-
white.

Fluorescence: The emission of a different wavelength of light than the one
absorbed. The gas in a fluorescent
tube gives off ultraviolet light, which is
absorbed by the tube's coating and
emitted as visible light.

Lumen: A measure of the power of a
given light as perceived by the human
eye. Since the eye is sensitive to some
wavelengths and not others, a lumen
does not measure the total power out-
put of the light.

Oculus: The Latin word for "eye." In a
lighting context, it is the name of the
round window at the top of a building
(such as the Parthenon in Rome) which
lets in light.

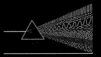

Full-Spectrum Light: Artificial light that
more closely mimics the color range of
sunlight, as opposed to yellow-rich
incandescent light or blue-rich fluorescent light.

Candlepower: The waxy oil from
sperm whales is so pure that candles
made from it burned with a uniform
brightness that other light sources
could be compared to, thus leading
to the old physics standard "one
candlepower."

Bioluminescence: Children all over the
world capture fireflies to use in lan-
terns. Now genetic engineers are
working to insert the insect's "glow"
genes into different living beings.
Imagine a houseplant that doubles as
a nightlight!

Smart Glass: Glass with embedded
liquid crystals that can be darkened
by the application of electricity. It can
be used to let the sun in on cold winter
days, but keep it out on hot summer
days.

September 2010

AN INTRODUCTION TO LIGHTING

by: Emmanuel Romeuf
for: Dwell magazine
in: USA

A series of illustrations for an article about the current revolution
in energy-efficient lighting for the
architecture and design magazine
Dwell. The article gives a short history of lighting in domestic architecture, starting with the manipula-
tion of sunlight up to the invention
of the light bulb and the current
move to light sources that consume
less energy. A primer explains old
and new light sources such as the
oculus window used in the ceiling
of the Parthenon and smart glass
that accepts or rejects sunlight depending on the season. The growing selection of energy-efficient
lighting provides consumers with
options that use less electricity and
provide the best illumination solution for specific spaces.

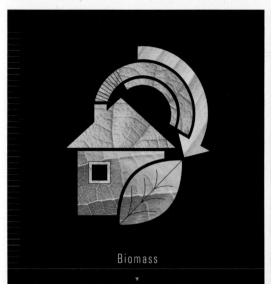

Biomass

Plants convert solar energy into chemical energy through the process of photosynthesis. Every organic substance that can be used as a source of energy is biomass. The first thing we obtain from biomass is heat, which can then be used for heating as well as for the production of electricity. Biomass is the most important renewable energy source in Slovenia. Today, biomass alone heats over 25% of Slovenian households.

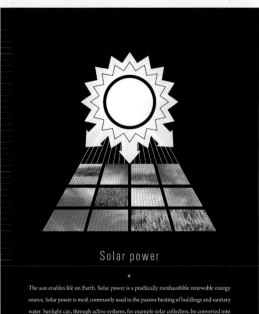

Solar power

The sun enables life on Earth. Solar power is a practically inexhaustible renewable energy source. Solar power is most commonly used in the passive heating of buildings and sanitary water. Sunlight can, through active systems, for example solar collectors, be converted into electricity. The use of solar power is growing strongly in Slovenia; between 2006 and 2007, there was a 10% growth in use.

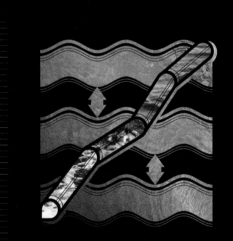

Wave power

Anyone who has ridden a surfboard knows how enormous the power of the waves can be. However, this type of energy is difficult to harness, which is why plants using wave power are few in number. The first commercial wind power plant is the Aguçadoura Wave Park in Portugal. Natural conditions in Slovenia do not allow the use of wave power.

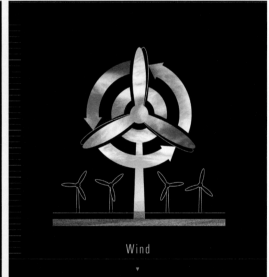

Wind

Man learned very early on how to harness the power of the wind. Wind powered the mills that turned wheat into flour and drove the ships that discovered the world. The first wind-powered electricity plants appeared around 1920. Not long ago there was a heated debate in Slovenia over the Volovja Reber wind farm; despite this, there are already several smaller wind farms in the country that are connected to the electricity grid.

SLOVENIAN INSURANCE BULLETIN 2009 ILLUSTRATIONS

by: Lukatarina
for: Slovenian Insurance Association
in: Slovenia and Europe

Insurance companies lose millions of euros due to changing weather conditions caused by global warming. Highlighting the fact that climate protection is really everyone's business, Lukatarina's series of illustrations for the *Statistical Insurance Bulletin* is all about renewable energy sources. Each visual is accompanied by an explanatory text, highlighting both possibilities and possible problems that alternative ways of energy generation brings about.

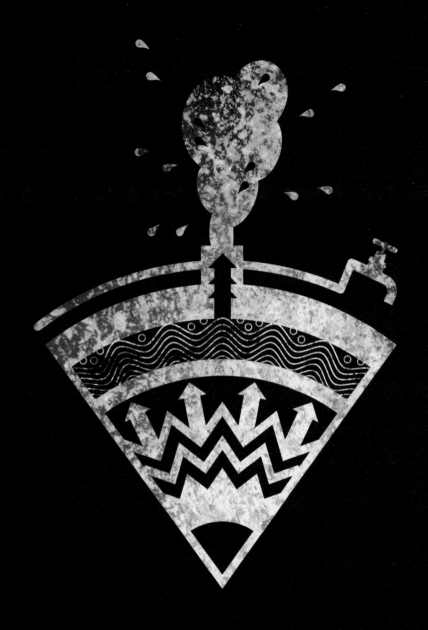

Geothermal energy

▼

The heat stored in the interior of the Earth is called geothermal energy. We can harness it in a number of ways. Hot water and steam springs were already familiar to the Romans. Today, geothermal energy is used in Slovenia to generate heat, mainly in natural health resorts. Heat pumps are increasingly being used. In Murska Sobota for example, thermal water is used for heating and for the preparation of sanitary water. There they save up to 2,000 tonnes of heating oil a year by using geothermal energy.

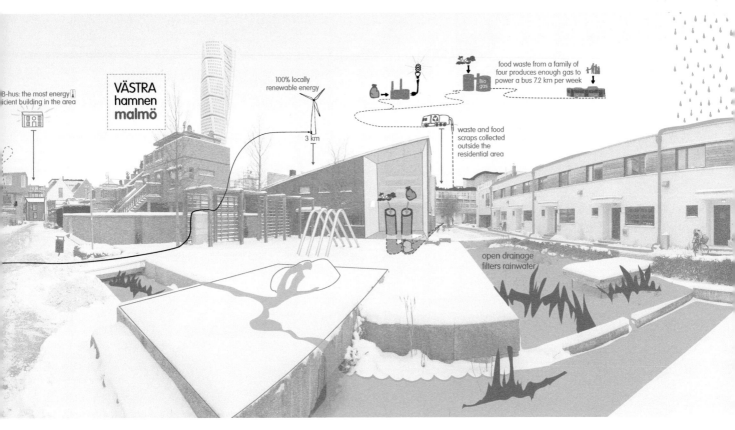

B-hus: the most energy
icient building in the area

VÄSTRA hamnen malmö

100% locally
renewable energy

3 km

food waste from a family of
four produces enough gas to
power a bus 7.2 km per week

Bio gas

waste and food
scraps collected
outside the
residential area

open drainage
filters rainwater

BEHIND-THE-SCENES PERISCOPE

by: Background Stories //
Arlene Birt
for: Artist residency at MEDEA
in: Malmö, Sweden

The American artist and information designer Arlene Birt created the **BEHIND-THE-SCENES PERISCOPE** during her artist residency at MEDEA in Malmö, Sweden. Inspired by the ecologically sustainable infrastructure of the Västra Hamnen section of the city, she created a 360-degree illustration viewed through a rotating periscope that shows the neighborhood's hidden energy-saving technologies. By overlaying the illustration onto the actual landscape, the viewer can connect behind-the-scenes elements to the larger system. The periscope was created with the interactive design studio Unsworn Industries, whose Parascope project allows people to see the future of Malmö's streets once automobile traffic has been reduced or eliminated.

A NEW PHOTOSYNTHETHIS

by: Jan von Holleben
for: Geo magazine
in: Berlin, Germany

Photos created for an article in the German magazine *Geo*. The article explores the idea of solving the planet's energy problem by creating a modern form of photosynthesis. Von Holleben's photographs combine real leaves and objects into absurd mechanical compositions to illustrate the master plans of three international scientists. Each holds a key to part of the photosynthesis solution—if they work together, they could make plants produce oxygen and glucose for industrial usage.

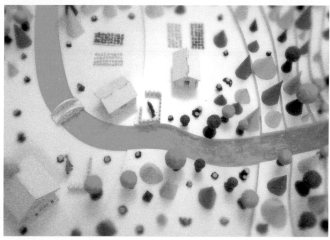

CÓDIGO FLORESTAL BRASILEIRO

by: Buraco de Bala //
    Aleixo Leite, Bruno Rojas, Emerson Rodrigues
for: WWF
in: Brasília, Brazil

When the Brazilian government announced a destructive new conservation policy, the World Wildlife Fund created a short film as a call to action. This one-minute spot aimed to educate the public about the new policy and urged them to pressure their political leaders into voting for the environment. Without being overbearing, the film condenses a serious and informative message into a small amount of time.

Seite 54
Vergleich

0,27 Euro ...

... kostete ein Liter bei der Einfuhr 2009.
Insgesamt wurden 113 488 372 000 Liter
Rohöl im Wert von 30,9 Milliarden Euro nach
Deutschland importiert

Unser Leben mit Öl

**Energieträger, Rohstoff, Umweltverschmutzer:
Hier zeigen wir, was aus einem Liter Erdöl alles
werden kann – und was er anzurichten vermag**

Als am 20. April die Plattform Deepwater Horizon in die Luft
flog und als Folge geschätzte 9,6 Millionen Liter Erdöl pro Tag
den Golf von Mexiko verunreinigten, war es wie immer bei einer Ölpest: Man wünschte sich, man könne endlich auf das kleb-
rige Zeug verzichten. Doch das ist (noch) undenkbar. Aus ihm
wird nicht nur Benzin für Fahrzeuge, Brennstoff für Heizungen,
sondern auch Kunststoff gemacht. Telefone, Spielzeug, Fernseh-
geräte, Teppichböden – in jedem Haushalt „stecken" durch-
schnittlich 150 Liter Erdöl. Ohne Öl keine Seifen, Parfüms, Au-
toreifen, Plastikflaschen, selbst die meisten Medikamente
enthalten es. Dabei verarbeitet die Kunststoffindustrie nur etwa
4 Prozent des geförderten Erdöls, 40 Prozent davon werden zu
Kraftstoffen und demnach irgendwann in die Luft geblasen. Be-
denkt man die Fördermenge von weltweit knapp 4,5 Billionen
Litern jährlich (2009), ist der Klimakollaps nur logisch. Auch
wenn aufgrund versiegender Quellen in 50 Jahren damit Schluss
sein soll: Bis dahin geht der Ölmissbrauch munter weiter. /

TEXT Christian Sobiella ILLUSTRATION Mattias Leutwyler

50 Prozent

Rund ein Liter Rohöl reicht aus, um 1000
Liter Meerwasser zu vergiften. Das zeigten
entsprechende Laborversuche, in denen
die Hälfte aller eingebrachten Fischlarven,
Fischeier und Krebse starben

0,46 Liter

Das ist etwa die Menge Benzin und Diesel,
die bei der so genannten Fraktion gewonnen
wird. Dabei wird ausgenutzt, dass die
verschiedenen Bestandteile des Öls bei
unterschiedlichen Graden sieden

QUELLEN uni-marburg.de, 3sat, Texas Oil, taz.de, ZEIT online, FCIÖ Chemische Industrie

0,57 kg

Etwas mehr als ein halbes Kilogramm
Fichtenholz hat den gleichen Brennwert wie
0,3 Liter Heizöl. Und um das zu gewinnen
ist ein Liter Erdöl notwendig

6,57 Kilometer

Soweit fährt ein Auto mit dem Sprit, der aus
einem Liter Öl gewonnen wird. 2010 verbrauchen Neuwagen in Deutschland im Schnitt
rund sieben Liter Kraftstoff auf 100 km

250 Gramm

In einem halben Pfund Gemüse oder Obst aus
Übersee steckt ein Liter Rohöl. Ursachen:
Gewächshäuser bauen und
beheizen, Transporte mit Schiff und Lkw,
Verpackungen aus Plastik

0,6 Cent

Das kostet (je nach aktuellem Weltölpreis)
ein Liter Rohöl direkt an der Quelle in
Kuwait. Enthalten sind schon die Kosten der
Suche, der Bohrungen oder der Förderung

60 Tonnen

Gewicht der Pflanzenmasse, die über
Millionen Jahre durch Druck, Hitze und
Bakterien zu einem Liter Erdöl wurde. In den
letzten 250 Jahren wurden von uns so viele
fossile Brennstoffe (also auch Gas) verbraucht, wie in 13 300 Jahren an Pflanzenmasse nachwachsen

1 000 000 Liter ...

... Trinkwasser werden durch einen Liter
Öl so ungenießbar, dass von dem Genuss
dringend abzuraten ist

GRAFIK
MIKROKREDITE

Der weltweite Fluss der Mikrokredite – so gelangt das Geld zu den Mikrokreditnehmern

Die in Mikrokredite investierten Finanzmittel stammen aus zwei großen Quellen. Dies sind zum einen die Einlagen der Sparer für Mikrofinanz-Institutionen, wie die der Fides Bank in Namibia. Zum anderen fließen den Mikrofinanz-Institutionen Gelder von Öffentlichen Anlegern (bsp. der KfW) sowie von institutionellen (bsp. Banken, Versicherungen, Pensionskassen) und privaten Anlegern (bsp. Unternehmen, NGOs und sozial motivierten Anlegern) zu. Dies geschieht teilweise direkt, teilweise mit dem Umweg über Staaten und sogenannte Mikrofinanz-Investment-Vehikel (bsp. Investmentfonds). Nach Schätzungen der CGAP (Consultative Group to Assist the Poor/Weltbank) sicherten bzw. hafteten Öffentliche, private und institutionelle Anleger im Jahr 2006 für rund 5 Milliarden Dollar; 3,9 Milliarden Dollar davon wurden tatsächlich an die Mikrokredit-Institutionen ausgeschüttet. Nach Angaben des Microfinance Information eXchange gaben weltweit fast 3000 Mikrokreditinstitute ihre Kredite an rund 86 Millionen Kreditnehmern aus. /

QUELLE Microfinance Information eXchange: Microfinance at a Glance 2008 (aktualisiert: 31.12.2009)/CGAP survey, 2006. Es wurden nicht alle Länder in den dargestellten Regionen erfasst.

Seite 30
Titel

Seite 31
Titel

2,60 Mrd $
Private und institutionelle Anleger

2,45 Mrd $
Öffentliche Anleger

Mikrofinanz-Vehikel

Staaten und Netzwerke

384 275 60 190 292 194

1341 $

14,1 Mio 526 $ 746 $ 912 $ 4008 $ 684 $

7,5 Mio 2,5 Mio 3,0 Mio

44,4 Mio 14,6 Mio

Länderkennung

- Lateinamerika / Karibik
- Afrika südlich der Sahara
- Mittlerer Osten / Nordafrika
- Südasien
- Osteuropa / Zentralasien
- Ostasien / Pazifik

In Mikrokredite investiertes Geld (in US-Dollar)

Durchschnittliche Mikrokredithöhe (in US-Dollar)

Anzahl der Mikrofinanz-institute weltweit

Anzahl Mikrokreditnehmer weltweit (haupts. Frauen)

ÖLVERGLEICH ^{previous page}

by: KONTEXTKOMMUNIKATION //
Carsten Hermann, Judith Hehl, Rike Noetzold
for: enorm Social Publish Verlag
in: Berlin, Germany

The German independent business magazine *enorm* postulates and promotes the social business approach in all of its facets. Claiming "business for the people," it addresses social difficulties in an engaging and aesthetically pleasing way. The illustration ÖLVERGLEICH (Oil Comparison) by KONTEXTKOMMUNIKATION is all about oil consumption and the tricky question, "What can be made of one liter of oil?" Rendered in watercolor, and in grungy tints that allude to oil slick, a set of startling responses is presented on a demonstrative double-page spread.

MIKROKREDITE

by: KONTEXTKOMMUNIKATION //
Carsten Hermann, Judith Hehl, Rike Noetzold
for: enorm Social Publish Verlag
in: Berlin, Germany

The small loans given to disadvantaged borrowers can help struggling entrepreneurs start businesses, raise themselves out of poverty, and contribute to their communities. KONTEXTKOMMUNIKATION's infographic for the socially and ecologically sensitive business magazine *enorm* visualizes the global flow of microcredit coming from two major sources: microfinance institutions and a mixture of public institutions and private investors. Tracing the global flow of money from its sources to those it is intended to help, the graphic highlights the disparity of initial sums and the final amounts loaned. A crafty three-dimensional thread illustration on the issue's cover picks up on the problem of financial dependency: Who holds the purse strings? The message is clear, without feeling dogmatic. In line with ENORM's sustainability-orientated approach the entire magazine — including the cover — is printed on ecological paper.

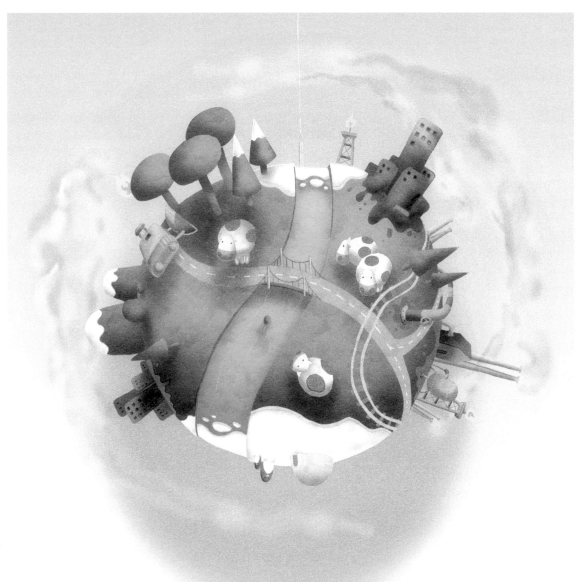

WORLD

by: Buraco de Bala //
    Aleixo Leite, Bruno Rojas,
    Emerson Rodrigues
for: WWF
in: Brasília, Brazil

WORLD is the first in a series of three short films exposing the process of global warming. It uses three-dimensional animation to show viewers the consequences of industrialized society's behavior on the environment; over a 30-second times-pan, the tiny rotating Earth goes from a green oasis to an overcrowded mess with a ring of pollution obstructing its view. With each rotation of the globe, trees and green space disappear. They are replaced by agriculture, buildings, and roads until they become only a tiny percentage of the earth's surface.

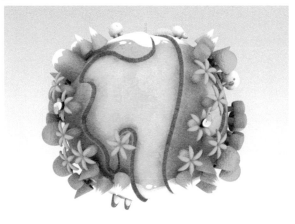

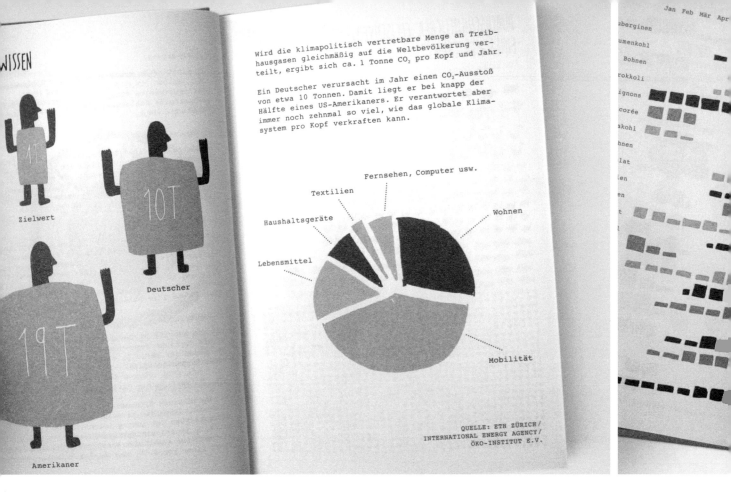

Zielwert

Deutscher

Amerikaner

Wird die klimapolitisch vertretbare Menge an Treibhausgasen gleichmäßig auf die Weltbevölkerung ver-
teilt, ergibt sich ca. 1 Tonne CO₂ pro Kopf und Jahr.

Ein Deutscher verursacht im Jahr einen CO₂-Ausstoß
von etwa 10 Tonnen. Damit liegt er bei knapp der
Hälfte eines US-Amerikaners. Er verantwortet aber
immer noch zehnmal so viel, wie das globale Klima-
system pro Kopf verkraften kann.

Textilien
Fernsehen, Computer usw.
Haushaltsgeräte
Wohnen
Lebensmittel
Mobilität

QUELLE: ETH ZÜRICH /
INTERNATIONAL ENERGY AGENCY /
ÖKO-INSTITUT E.V.

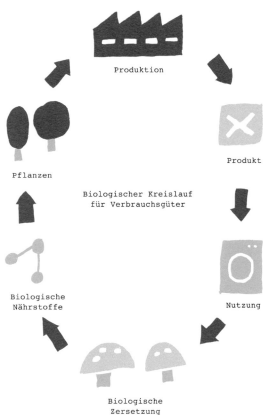

Produktion

Produkt

Biologischer Kreislauf
für Verbrauchsgüter

Pflanzen

Nutzung

Biologische
Nährstoffe

Biologische
Zersetzung

TO COVER VOL. 3

by: JUNO Hamburg //
Sebastian Schneider, Björn Lux
for: peyer graphic ag
in: Germany

JUNO designed a promotional notebook
series for peyer graphic that focuses on
environmental topics such as infinite
energy resources, new materials, and
carbon emissions. It provides designers—and everyone else—with ideas
for sustainable practices like a season-
able vegetable calendar and the biological circuit for consumer goods. The
book is for reading and reference, but
most of all for inspiration.

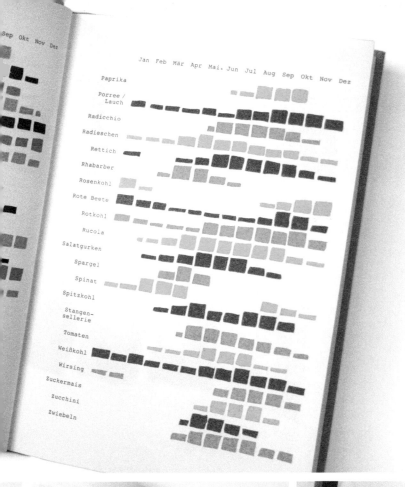

	Jan	Feb	Mär	Apr	Mai.	Jun	Jul	Aug	Sep	Okt	Nov	Dez
Paprika												
Porree / Lauch												
Radicchio												
Radieschen												
Rettich												
Rhabarber												
Rosenkohl												
Rote Beete												
Rotkohl												
Rucola												
Salatgurken												
Spargel												
Spinat												
Spitzkohl												
Stangen-sellerie												
Tomaten												
Weißkohl												
Wirsing												
Zuckermais												
Zucchini												
Zwiebeln												

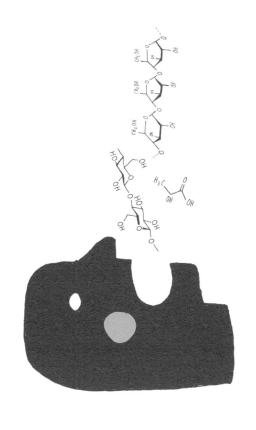

PLANT MORE FLOWERS

IDEEN

KLIMA / WISSEN

Treibhauseffekt

In der Atmosphäre angesammelte Treibhausgase ver-hindern die Wärmerückstrahlung von der Erde ins All. Die natürliche Konzentration dieser Gase in der Atmosphäre sorgt dafür, dass auf der Erde eine durchschnittliche Temperatur von 15°C herrscht. Der zusätzliche Ausstoß von Treibhausgasen durch den Menschen heizt das Klima weiter auf und produziert einen Klimawandel mit schwerwiegenden Folgen (u.a. Anstieg des Meeresspiegels, Verschiebung der Klima-zonen, Zunahme von Stürmen).

Treibhausgase

Die wichtigsten Treibh... (CO_2), Methan (CH_4), Dis... teilhalogenierte Fluor... perfluorierte Kohlenwass... hexafluorid (SF_6).

CO_2-Äquivalent

Hinsichtlich seiner Trei... Treibhausgas auf Kohlend... werden. 1 kg Methan (CH_4) w... CO_2-Äquivalent entspreche... dazu, die weiteren Treibha... Zielerfüllung ebenfalls zu...

Ökologischer Fußabdruck

Der ökologische Fußabdruck... cenverbrauch. Er bezieht si... fähigkeit des Systems Erde ... Biokapazität gemessen in He... den muss, um die Ressourcen ... Region, einen Haushalt oder ... stellen und ihre Abfälle auf...

CO_2-Neutralität

Mit dem Begriff CO_2-Neutralitä... werden Zustände beziehungswei... bei denen das aktuelle globale ... nicht verändert wird.

Klimaneutralität (durch Kompens...

Man spricht von Klimaneutralitä... einem Ort durch die Vermeidung d... einem anderen Ort ausgeglichen we... Erzielte Emissionsreduktionen we... zertifikaten verbrieft. Dabei ent... fikat einer Tonne CO_2 oder CO_2-Äqui...

2007–2008 IBM CORPORATE RESPONSIBILITY REPORT

by: VSA Partners //
Curt Schreiber, Claudine Litman,
Brandt Brinkerhoff

for: IBM

Understanding corporate responsibility and ecological awareness as key aspects of contemporary entrepreneurialism, IBM commissioned VSA Partners to design a report that would communicate their business strategy and serve as an educational guidebook for good citizenship at the same time. Presenting itself as a 21st-century encyclopedia, the resulting Corporate Responsibility Report compiles a variety of bright, entertainingly illustrated stories and revealing infographics.

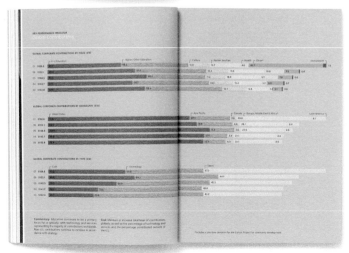

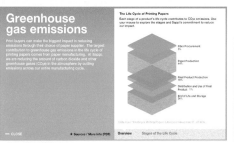

Greenhouse gas emissions

The Life Cycle of Printing Papers

Carbon offsets

Sustainably harvested wood

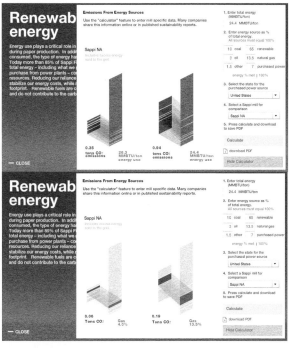

Renewable energy

Emissions From Energy Sources

Minimize waste

Recycled fiber

Renewable energy

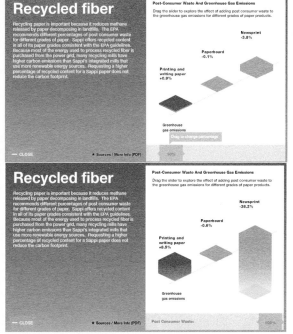

Recycled fiber

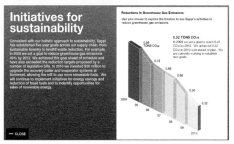

Initiatives for sustainability

EQ TOOL

by: IDEO
for: Sappi Fine Paper
     North America
in: Boston, USA

The EQ TOOL is an interactive website that informs about the environmental impact of paper manufacturing. Commissioned by Sappi Fine Paper North America, IDEO developed a concept and design that allows users to understand how a responsible choice of a paper supplier affects the carbon footprint of a publication. Visitors to the site are encouraged to engage in a meaningful dialog with print industry stakeholders, and learn about and actively discuss key issues of the trade, like energy use, waste reduction, and the inclusion of recycled fiber in new products. There is also information on further contributing factors, such as greenhouse gas emissions, renewable energies, managing process that are employed to minimize waste, carbon offsets, or sustainably-harvested wood. Sappi customers can use the EQ TOOL to generate a customized product statement that summarizes the environmental benefits of choosing Sappi Fine Paper North America's papers for their print job.

If the world were a village of 100 people

ENERGY

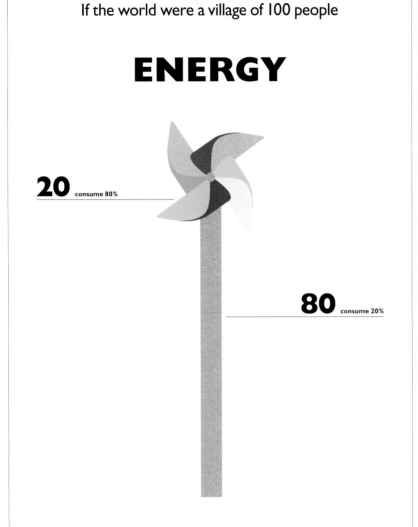

20 consume 80%

80 consume 20%

If the world were a village of 100 people

AIR

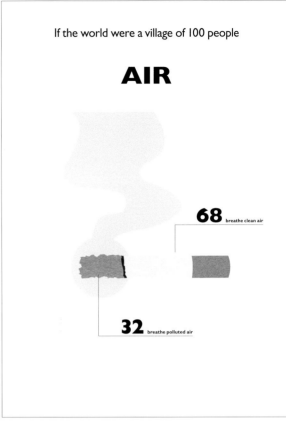

68 breathe clean air

32 breathe polluted air

THE WORLD OF 100 POSTCARDS

by: Toby Ng Design // Toby Ng

in: Hong Kong

In 2008, graphic designer Toby Ng gathered statistics about the world's population and turned the numbers into a series of 20 postcards that posed the question: If the world were a village of 100 people, what would its environmental and social landscapes look like? Each postcard addresses a different topic such as energy, air, religion, and water. The topics are illustrated with colorful and simple images such as a flame for religion, a pinwheel for energy, a cigarette for air. Corresponding statistics are represented by inhabitants of Ng's global village. The result is a message of urgency and compassion that is easy to grasp because of its human scale. The series was awarded the 2009 red dot award for communication design, and an updated series was released in 2011.

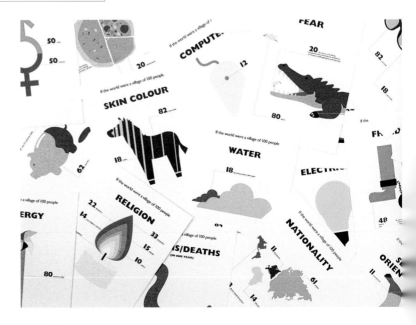

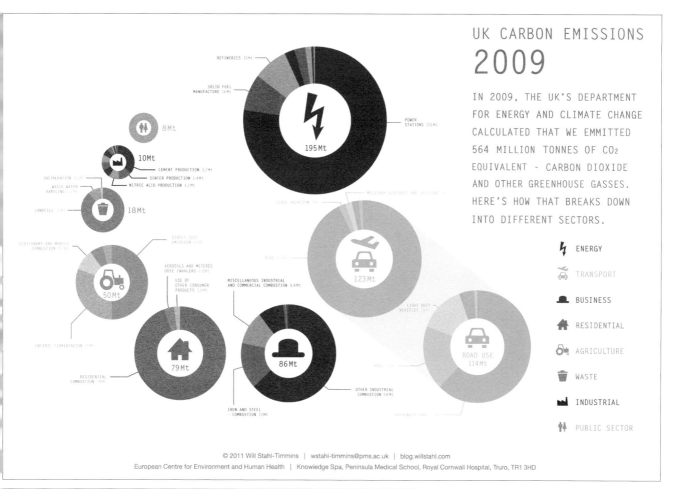

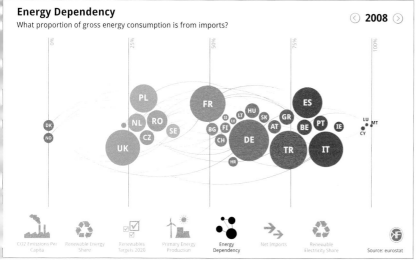

UK CARBON EMISSIONS 2009

by: European Centre for the Environment
& Human Health, Will Stahl-Timmins
for: Personal project
in: Truro, U.K.

After seeing the 2009 carbon emissions data for the United Kingdom, information designer Will Stahl-Timmins was struck by the enormous contribution personal transportation makes to the final number. He created an infographic illustrating the point that while public energy policy is important, the environmental impact of the passenger car should not be underestimated. Governments, businesses, and individuals all need to play a part in reducing greenhouse gas emissions.

EUROPE'S ENERGY

by: Gregor Aisch
for: Open Knowledge Foundation
in: Germany

To reduce greenhouse gas emissions, EU member states agreed on set goals that will cut energy consumption and increase renewable energy use by the year 2020. The EUROPE'S ENERGY project put these goals into context with an interactive infographic that clearly shows how EU countries produce and consume their energy. Each category — CO2 emissions per capita, renewable energy share, renewables targets, primary energy production, energy dependency, net imports, and renewable elecricity share — can be viewed according to year from 1998 to 2008. EUROPE'S ENERGY was featured in the *Guardian* and won a silver award at Malofiej 20, which recognizes innovative infographics from around the world.

Smart Grid

1. Kraftwerke

2. Virtuelle Kraftwerke

3. Schalt-/Steuerzentrale

4. Smarter Stromzähler

5. Private Erzeuger

6. Erneuerbare Energien

7. Stromspeicher

Problem:
Heftige Stürme und schmelzendes Eis in der Arktis, Wüstenbildung und Hochwasser – der weltweite Temperaturanstieg hat weitreichende Folgen.

Smart Grid:
1.) Herkömmliche Kraftwerke liefern derzeit noch die größte Menge Elektrizität, sind aber schwerfällig und können kaum auf kurzfristige Schwankungen bei Einspeisung und Entnahme von Strom reagieren. — 2.) Kleine, oft in Privathaushalten installierte Kraftwerke können – als »Schwarm« zusammengeschaltet – beachtliche Energiemengen flexibel ins Stromnetz einspeisen. — 3.) Als Bindeglied zwischen Erzeugern und Verbrauchern verwalten und optimieren die Schalt- und Steuerzentralen der Smart Grids den vielfältigen Zu- und Abfluss von elektrischem Strom in den Versorgungsnetzen. — 4.) »Intelligente« Zähler bei den Verbrauchern regeln, zu welchen Zeiten welche Geräte laufen und nutzen so nicht nur den günstigsten Strom, sondern sichern auch die gleichmäßige und effektive Auslastung der Netze. — 5.) Haushalte konsumieren nicht nur Strom, sondern können ihn etwa durch Solarkollektoren auch erzeugen. — 6.) Wind-, Solar-, Wasser- und Gezeitenkraftwerke liefern keinen kontinuierlichen Strom, weil ihre Energieerzeugung natürlichen Schwankungen unterliegt. Intelligente Netze regeln die Einspeisung des gewonnenen Stroms. — 7.) Elektromobilität bietet die Möglichkeit, in Spitzenzeiten Strom in die Fahrbatterien einzuspeisen und ihn bei Bedarf wieder ins Netz zurückzugeben. Ergänzend dazu sind auch stationäre Stromspeicher (Batterieprinzip) in der Entwicklung.

Text: Klaus Jopp, DB Mobil — Design made in United States of the Art

SMART GRID ^{opposite page}

by: United States of the Art //
Carsten Raffel
for: DB Mobil
in: Hamburg, Germany

An infographic about networked energy for Deutsche Bahn's customer magazine. The article explores the smart grid as a solution to inefficient energy consumption and climate change; it can improve efficiency, regulate supply and demand, avoid outages, save money, and provide incentives for participants to consume energy more efficiently. The design juxtaposes the violent storms, Arctic melting, desertification, and flooding caused by climate change with a diagram of the smart grid. Each section of the smart grid is an icon, connected by directional arrows explaining its relationship to the system as a whole.

HOW TO SAVE THE CLIMATE—JOIN THE ENERGY (R)EVOLUTION

by: United States of the Art //
Carsten Raffel
for: Greenpeace International
in: Hamburg, Germany

Tips for saving energy and reducing CO_2 emissions were translated into a set of multilingual brochures with accompanying pictograms. Created in partnership with the design studio Büro Hamburg, the international campaign required iconic illustrations that could convey complex messages without relying on language. Good practices such as unplugging computer and phone chargers at night and taking short showers instead of baths are rendered with bright colors and simple imagery in a design that clearly delivers a serious message with engaging images that can be understood by anyone.

44 TIPPS ZUM STROMSPAREN

SIE WOLLEN ÖKOSTROM VON GREENPEACE ENERGY?
→ RUFEN SIE AN: **040 / 808 110 - 600,** → ODER WECHSELN SIE ONLINE: **WWW.GREENPEACE-ENERGY.DE**

LAMPEN, LICHT UND LEERLAUF

DIE **BELEUCHTUNG** MACHT ETWA ACHT PROZENT DES STROMVERBRAUCHS IN DEUTSCHEN HAUSHALTEN AUS.

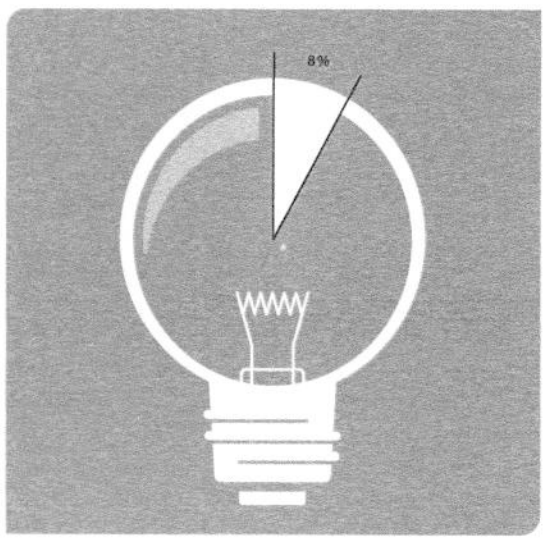

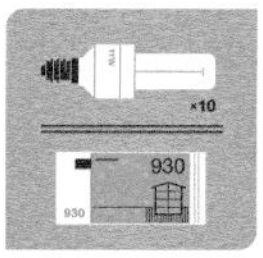

1 → Wenn Sie zehn 60-Watt-Lampen durch Elf-Watt-Sparlampen ersetzen, sparen Sie trotz höherer Anschaffungskosten in zehn Jahren rund 930 Euro. Eine **Energiesparlampe** verbraucht bis zu 80 Prozent weniger Strom als eine Glühbirne und hält etwa zehnmal länger. Sparlampen gibt's in verschiedenen Lichtfarben, Formen und Größen. Hochwertige Sparlampen überstehen problemlos häufiges Ein- und Ausschalten. Eine Übersicht bietet www.ecotopten.de/prod_lampen_prod.php

2 → Leuchtstofflampen, auch **Neonröhren** genannt, halten 10.000 Betriebsstunden oder mehr und verbrauchen 75 Prozent weniger Strom als normale Glühlampen. Sie eignen sich besonders gut für Keller-, Hauswirtschafts- oder Hobbyräume. Achtung: Ausgediente Leuchtstoff- und Energiesparlampen enthalten geringe Mengen Quecksilber. Deshalb beim Wertstoffhof oder der Schadstoffsammelstelle abgeben.

3 → Niedervolt-**Halogenlampen** verbrauchen weniger als Glühbirnen, sind aber keine eigentlichen Sparlampen. Sie haben oft einen Transformator, der auch nach dem Ausschalten Strom braucht. Das erkennen Sie daran, dass der Trafo nach dem Abschalten warm bleibt, brummt oder ein Anzeigelämpchen leuchtet. Einfachste Lösung: Stecker ziehen oder abschaltbare Steckdosenleiste nutzen.

4 → Wenn bei Ihnen eine Renovierung ansteht: Die Gestaltung von Haus oder Wohnung hat Einfluss auf Ihren Stromverbrauch. So wirken **hell gestrichene und möblierte Räume** ohne schwere, Licht schluckende Vorhänge nicht nur freundlich, sondern helfen auch beim Energiesparen.

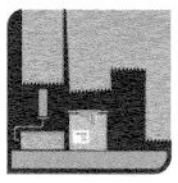

DER **STAND-BY-BETRIEB** VON ELEKTROGERÄTEN SCHLUCKT IN DEUTSCHLAND SO VIEL STROM, WIE ZWEI GROSSKRAFTWERKE PRODUZIEREN. DAS ENTSPRICHT DEM BEDARF DER 3,4-MILLIONEN-STADT BERLIN. DIE LEERLAUFVERLUSTE SUMMIEREN SICH AUF VIER PROZENT DES STROMVERBRAUCHS DEUTSCHER HAUSHALTE.

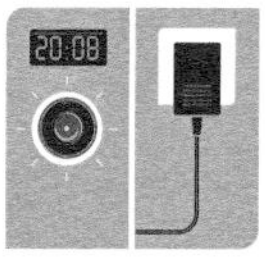

5 → Geräte im Stand-by-Modus können Sie häufig an **Kontrolllämpchen,** Zeitanzeigen oder Trafos erkennen, die bei Nichtgebrauch warm bleiben oder brummen.

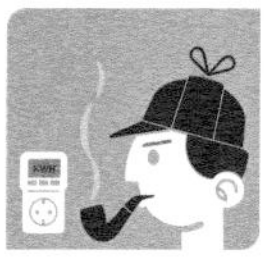

6 → Leerlaufverlusten durch Stand-by können Sie auch durch ein **Strommessgerät** auf die Spur kommen. Greenpeace Energy verleiht die Geräte kostenlos: 040 / 808 110 - 330 oder www.greenpeace-energy.de.

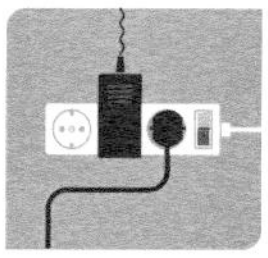

7 → Am besten ist es, schon beim Kauf Geräte zu wählen, die sich vollständig vom Netz trennen lassen. Sonst gilt: Bei Nichtgebrauch Netzstecker ziehen. Auch mit einer **abschaltbaren Steckdosenleiste** verhindern Sie, dass Geräte nach der Benutzung weiterhin Strom verbrauchen.

8 → So genannte **Power-Safer** registrieren den Stand-by-Zustand und schalten das Gerät nach einiger Zeit selbsttätig ab. Neuere Fernseher, Recorder, Musikanlagen, Rechner, Kopierer und Faxe zeigen mit dem GEEA-Energiesparzeichen, dass sie mit 0,1 bis 1 Watt für den Stand-by-Betrieb auskommen. Infos bei www.energielabel.de

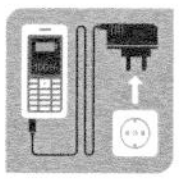

9 → Handy- und Akku-Ladegeräte, Radionetzteile, Satellitenreceiver und Halogenlampen sind heimliche Stromfresser. Zwei simple Griffe machen damit Schluss: einfach nach Gebrauch **Stecker ziehen** oder eine abschaltbare Steckerleiste zwischenschalten.

RÖHREN, RECHNER UND RECORDER

GERÄTE DER **UNTERHALTUNGSELEKTRONIK** WIE FERNSEHER, STEREOANLAGE, VIDEORECORDER ODER COMPUTER SIND FÜR ZEHN BIS 25 PROZENT DES STROMVERBRAUCHS IN DEUTSCHEN HAUSHALTEN VERANTWORTLICH.

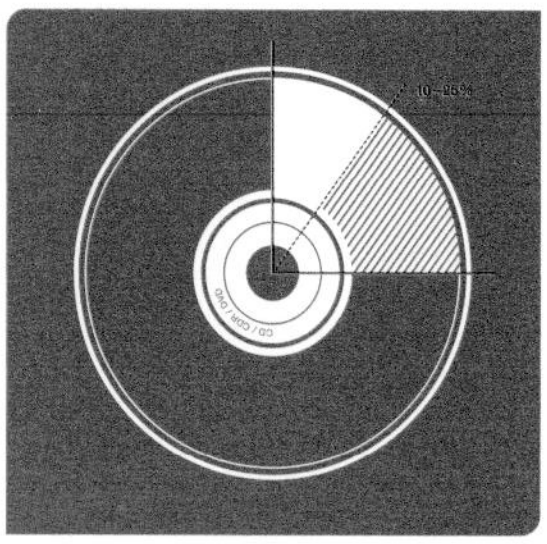

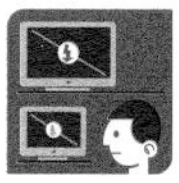

10 → Gut zu wissen beim Kauf eines Fernsehgeräts: Röhren- und **LCD-Fernseher** verbrauchen etwa gleich viel Strom, Plasmageräte fast doppelt so viel wie LCD-Modelle. Je größer Bildschirmdiagonale und Auflösung, desto höher meist auch der Stromverbrauch.

11 → **Kontrast und Helligkeit** sind ab Werk oft zu hoch eingestellt, das kostet unnötig Strom und lässt sich leicht regulieren.

12 → **Notebooks** sind sparsamer als Desktop-PCs. Aber auch da gibt es Unterschiede: Ein energieeffizienter Durchschnitts-PC verbraucht rund 75 Watt, ein sehr leistungsfähiger High-End-PC bis zu 300 Watt. Das schlägt bei täglich vier Stunden Nutzung mit 20 bis 90 Euro Mehrkosten jährlich zu Buche. Es zahlt sich also aus, gründlich zu überlegen, ob man wirklich alle verfügbaren Anwendungen braucht – und sich beim Neukauf über den Stromverbrauch zu informieren.

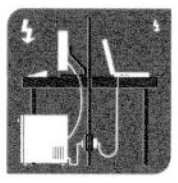

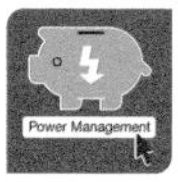

13 → Ein TFT-**Monitor** frisst so viel Strom wie der eigentliche Rechner, ein Röhrengerät gar das Doppelte. Auch Drucker, Scanner oder Lautsprecher verbrauchen viel. Abschalten lohnt schon bei kleinen Arbeitspausen.

14 → Moderne PCs haben eine Energiesparfunktion, genannt **Power Management,** die meist erst aktiviert werden muss. So verbrauchen nur die Hardware-Komponenten Strom, die gerade genutzt werden.

KOCHEN, KÜHLEN, KÖRPERPFLEGE

KOCHEN UND BACKEN MACHEN 17 PROZENT DES STROMVERBRAUCHS EINES DURCHSCHNITTSHAUSHALTS AUS.

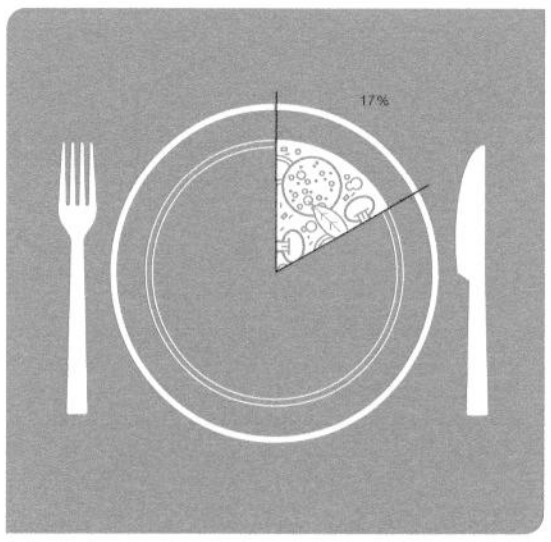

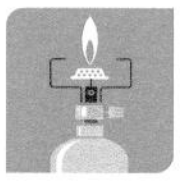

15 → Am besten und energieeffizientesten kocht es sich mit **Gas** – Profiköche wissen das. Der Elektroherd wandelt nur rund 34 Prozent der im Kraftwerk eingesetzten Energie in Strom um. Ein Ceranfeld spart gegenüber Gussplatten zehn bis 20 Prozent, ein Induktionsherd rund 30 Prozent Strom. Für Letzteren braucht man allerdings passendes Kochgeschirr.

16 → Energie sparen mit dem richtigen **Kochgeschirr:** Wärmeisolierte Töpfe senken den Stromverbrauch um etwa 15 Prozent. Töpfe und Pfannen sollten in der Größe genau der Kochplatte entsprechen, einen planen Boden haben und vor allem einen Deckel. Wenn der gut drauf ist, spart er gegenüber dem Kochen im offenen Topf bis zu 65 Prozent Strom. Durch einen Glasdeckel kann man in den Topf gucken, ohne ihn zu öffnen.

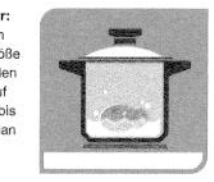

17 → Beim Garen sparen: Je **weniger Wasser,** desto geringer der Energieaufwand. Die Restwärme wird durch das Abschalten von Kochplatte oder Backofen fünf Minuten vor Ende der Garzeit optimal genutzt. Mit einem Dampfkochtopf können Sie bei einer Garzeit von mehr als 40 Minuten bis zu 50 Prozent Energie einsparen. Sehr effizient ist auch ein Thermokochtopf, den man nach der Hälfte der Kochzeit in eine Styroporkiste setzt, oder „Omas Kochkiste", ein wärmegedämmter Behälter, in dem die Speisen nach dem Ankochen ohne Wärmezufuhr weitergaren.

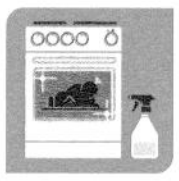

18 → Backen ohne Vorheizen spart bis zu 20 Prozent Energie. Die Scheibe der Backofentür sollte immer schön **sauber** sein, damit sie während des Backvorgangs möglichst selten geöffnet werden muss.

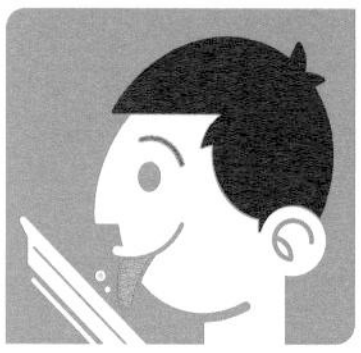

19 → Eine voll beladene **große Geschirrspülmaschine** braucht pro Gedeck weniger Energie als eine kleine für nur acht bis neun Gedecke. Das Aufheizen kostet den meisten Strom. Ein Kurz- oder Sparprogramm mit 50 Grad Celsius Wassertemperatur spart gegenüber einem Normalprogramm mit 65 Grad etwa 20 Prozent Energie und Wasser und reicht meist völlig aus. Das Geschirr sollte gut von Essensresten gereinigt, aber nicht vorgespült werden.

20 → Einen Liter Wasser erhitzen kostet im **Wasserkocher** rund zwei Cent, auf dem Elektroherd etwa 3,5 und in der Mikrowelle fünf Cent. Am günstigsten ist der Gasherd mit nur etwa 1,7 Cent.

21 → Die **Mikrowelle** ist unschlagbar kostengünstig für das Aufwärmen kleinerer Mengen (bis zu zwei Portionen).

22 → Zum Aufbacken von Brötchen eignet sich der **Toaster** oder Kleingrill besser als der Backofen, der verbraucht nämlich drei- bis viermal so viel Energie.

23 → Eine **Thermoskanne** hält günstiger warm als die Heizplatte der Kaffeemaschine und schont überdies das Aroma.

KÜHL- UND GEFRIERGERÄTE BENÖTIGEN ETWA 20 PROZENT DES STROMS, DEN DEUTSCHE HAUSHALTE VERBRAUCHEN.

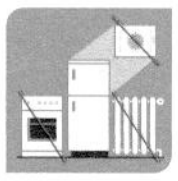

24 → Kühl- und Gefriergeräte fühlen sich in **kühler Umgebung** am wohlsten, Gefriergeräte können auch gut im Keller stehen. Auf keinen Fall sollten sie neben Heizung, Herd, Geschirrspüler oder Waschmaschine aufgestellt werden und auch nicht direkter Sonneneinstrahlung ausgesetzt sein. Eine um ein Grad Celsius niedrigere Raumtemperatur spart ungefähr drei Prozent Strom bei Gefrier- und sogar sechs Prozent bei Kühlgeräten.

25 → Kühlgeräte der **Effizienzklasse A++** verbrauchen nur halb so viel Strom wie A-Geräte. Bei Klasse A+ ist es immerhin rund ein Viertel weniger.

26 → Wenn nur noch Platz neben dem Herd ist, hilft ein zwischen den Geräten angebrachter **feuerfester Dämmstoff** gegen die Hitzeeinwirkung.

27 → Kalt ja, **Eiszeit nein:** Eine Kühlschranktemperatur von sieben Grad reicht völlig aus (minus 18 Grad beim Gefriergerät). Das spart im Vergleich zu einer Temperatur von fünf Grad etwa 15 Prozent Strom.

28 → Wer schon ein Gefriergerät besitzt, kann beim Kühlschrank **auf ein Dreisternefach verzichten.**

29 → Ein großer Kühlschrank im Singlehaushalt hat auch einen entsprechend enormen Strombedarf. Als Richtschnur für die Größe gilt ein Volumen von 60 Liter Nutzinhalt pro Person. Ein zu **70 Prozent gefüllter Kühlschrank** arbeitet am effizientesten.

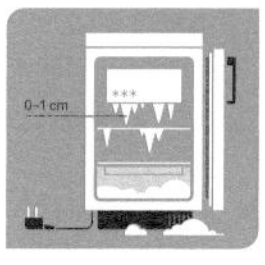

30 → Ein paar coole Kniffe helfen Strom sparen: Gefrorene Lebensmittel dürfen im Kühlschrank auftauen, erhitzte Speisen dagegen haben erst Zutritt, wenn sie abgekühlt sind. Das regelmäßige **Abtauen** (spätestens wenn die Eisschicht etwa einen Zentimeter dick ist) ist ebenso wichtig wie ein freies und sauberes Lüftungsgitter.

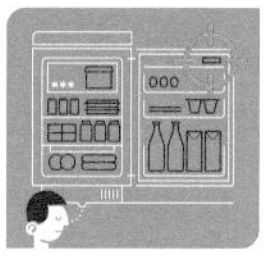

31 → Durch häufiges Öffnen der Kühlschranktür entweicht Kälte, was durch höheren Energieaufwand ausgeglichen werden muss. Diesen Kälteverlust können Sie reduzieren, indem Sie **vorher überlegen,** was sie brauchen. Enorm hilfreich ist dabei eine gewisse Ordnung!

32 → **Duschen** spart gegenüber Baden nicht nur 70 Liter Wasser, sondern auch Strom, wenn das Wasser elektrisch erwärmt wird.

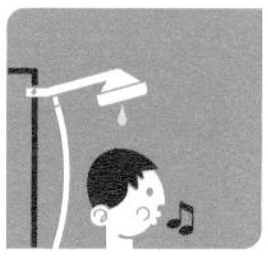

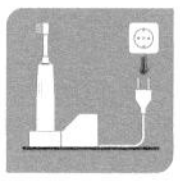

33 → Bis zu vier Leute können mit einer **elektrischen Zahnbürste** (und Wechsel-Bürstenköpfen) zweimal täglich Zähne putzen, ohne dass der Akku schlapp macht. Je seltener die Bürste läuft, desto häufiger sollte man den Stecker der Ladestation ziehen. Das spart Energie und verlängert auch die Lebensdauer des Geräts. Einzelnutzer brauchen nur einmal pro Woche 14 Stunden laden und können ansonsten mit Akku-Leistung putzen. Das reduziert den Stromverbrauch auf ein Siebtel.

34 → Wenn Sie sich elektrisch rasieren, spart ein Gerät **mit direktem Netzanschluss** im Vergleich zu Akku-Rasierern Strom.

WASCHEN, WÄRMEN, WERKELN

FÜRS **WÄSCHE WASCHEN** WERDEN IN DEUTSCHLAND JÄHRLICH 330 MILLIONEN KUBIKMETER WASSER UND ACHT MILLIARDEN KILOWATTSTUNDEN STROM BENÖTIGT. DAS ENTSPRICHT ACHT PROZENT DES STROMVERBRAUCHS IN DEUTSCHEN HAUSHALTEN.

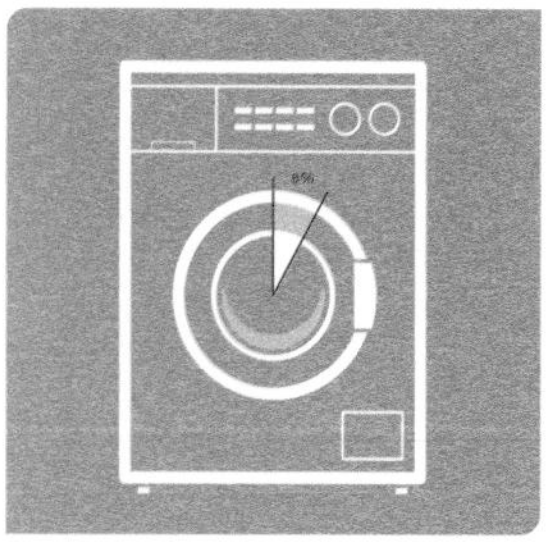

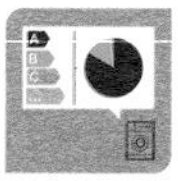

35 → Bei Waschmaschinen lohnt es sich, auch innerhalb der **Effizienzklasse** A auf die Unterschiede beim Stromverbrauch zu achten, denn rund 83 Prozent aller Geräte gehören in diese Kategorie (Stand 2005). Nur noch 15 Prozent der Geräte haben die Klasse B, die Klasse C spielt mit zwei Prozent inzwischen kaum noch eine Rolle. Klasse A verbraucht rund 40 Prozent weniger Strom als Klasse C.

36 → Egal ob Ihre Waschmaschine voll oder halb leer läuft: Der Strom- und Wasserverbrauch ändert sich kaum. Unterm Strich sparen Sie also richtig viel Energie, wenn Sie die Maschine **immer voll beladen.**

37 → Manche Maschinen haben die **Einstellung „1/2"**. Die verbraucht aber nicht, wie man glauben könnte, die Hälfte des Stroms, sondern verringert den Energiebedarf lediglich um rund ein Drittel.

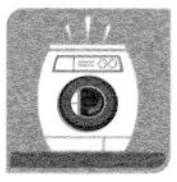

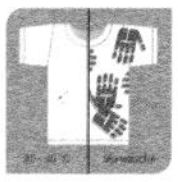

38 → Ein Kochwaschgang frisst siebenmal mehr Strom als 30-Grad-Wäsche und das Doppelte eines 60-Grad-Waschgangs. **Normal verschmutzte Wäsche** wird auch bei 30 Grad sauber. Vorwaschen lohnt nur bei extremer Verschmutzung.

39 → Das passende Programm ist leichter auszuwählen, wenn die Wäsche nach Farbe und Art **vorsortiert** ist und Flecken vorbehandelt worden sind.

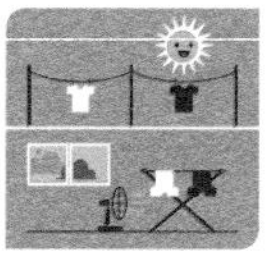

40 → Der beste und billigste Wäschetrockner ist die **Sonne.** Ein Garten ist dafür der schönste Platz, aber auch ein Trockenraum im Haus erfüllt seinen Zweck. Ein 25-Watt-Ventilator hilft, die Wäsche schneller zu trocknen.

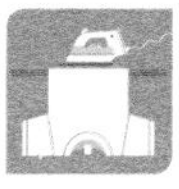

41 → Geht es nicht ohne Trockner, dann lautet Devise Nummer 1: **Gut geschleudert** ist halb getrocknet – das heißt, mit etwa 1.200 bis 1.400 Umdrehungen pro Minute. Devise Nummer 2: Bloß nicht zu viel des Guten tun und „übertrocknen". Wenn sowieso noch gebügelt werden muss, reicht „bügeltrocken".

42 → **Akku-Bohrschrauber** und andere kabellose Elektro-Werkzeuge stehen meist ungenutzt in ihrer Ladestation im Hobbykeller – und verbrauchen kontinuierlich weiter Strom. Dabei dauert Aufladen maximal einen Tag. Danach am besten Stecker ziehen.

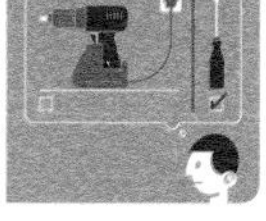

WÄRME: VIELE HEIZUNGEN SIND WAHRE ENERGIEFRESSER. DASS SIE DABEI AUSSER ÖL ODER GAS AUCH STROM VERBRAUCHEN, IST RELATIV UNBEKANNT. DIE HEIZUNGSPUMPE SCHLUCKT RUND ACHT PROZENT DES GESAMTVERBRAUCHS EINES HAUSHALTES.

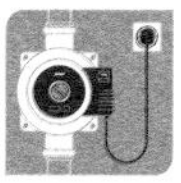

43 → Die Leistung der Heizungspumpe ist häufig zu großzügig eingestellt – wer sie auf eine niedrigere Stufe ein- und je nach Heizbedarf nachts ganz ausschaltet, kann den Stromverbrauch um mehr als ein Drittel senken. Für Einfamilienhäuser gibt es bereits **effiziente Umwälzpumpen,** die mit sechs bis 25 Watt Leistungsaufnahme (gegenüber 60 bis 100 Watt bei den alten Modellen) auskommen.

44 → Wer kann, sollte auf die elektrische Warmwasserbereitung verzichten und auf Gas, Fernwärme oder Solarkollektoren umrüsten. Warmwasserboiler verbrauchen im Dauerbetrieb Strom; ein **Thermo-Stopp** schaltet elektrische Warmwasserspeicher automatisch bei Erreichen der eingestellten Temperatur ab. Kleine Elektroboiler lassen sich über Nacht problemlos mit einer Zeitschaltuhr abschalten.

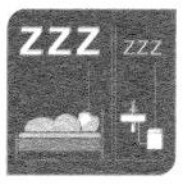

WWW.GREENPEACE-ENERGY.DE

by: United States of the Art //
    Carsten Raffel
for: Greenpeace Energy eG
in: Hamburg, Germany

This larger version of the original brochure **44 TIPPS ZUM STROM-SPAREN** (44 Tips for Saving Energy) was designed as a wall poster to be used as a daily reference for running a more energy-efficient household. Simple but detailed graphics address energy problems and solutions in a clever and humorous way by dividing the potentially overwhelming number of tips into four color-coded sections. Each section corresponds to an area or activity in the home: lighting, computers and televisions, kitchen and bathroom, washing and heating.

POLAR MELTDOWN
Effects on The United States' East and Gulf Coasts

POLAR MELTDOWN

by: The Ohio State University //
    Amanda Buck
in: Columbus, USA

The profound effects of melting polar ice on coastal areas and their inhabitants can be hard to grasp. The infographic **POLAR MELTDOWN** highlights the coastline of the eastern United States that would be submerged as a result of rising ocean levels, including facts about how arctic melting occurs and the indirect effects of rising ocean levels on public health and geography. Densely populated areas of the coastline are enlarged for a detailed view of what would be lost, such as the World Trade Center Memorial and the city of Miami. By calling out the vulnerability of well-known landmarks and cities, the hope is to impart an emotional understanding of the consequences of global warming. Designed as a poster, the format can educate pedestrians about the urgency of the issue.

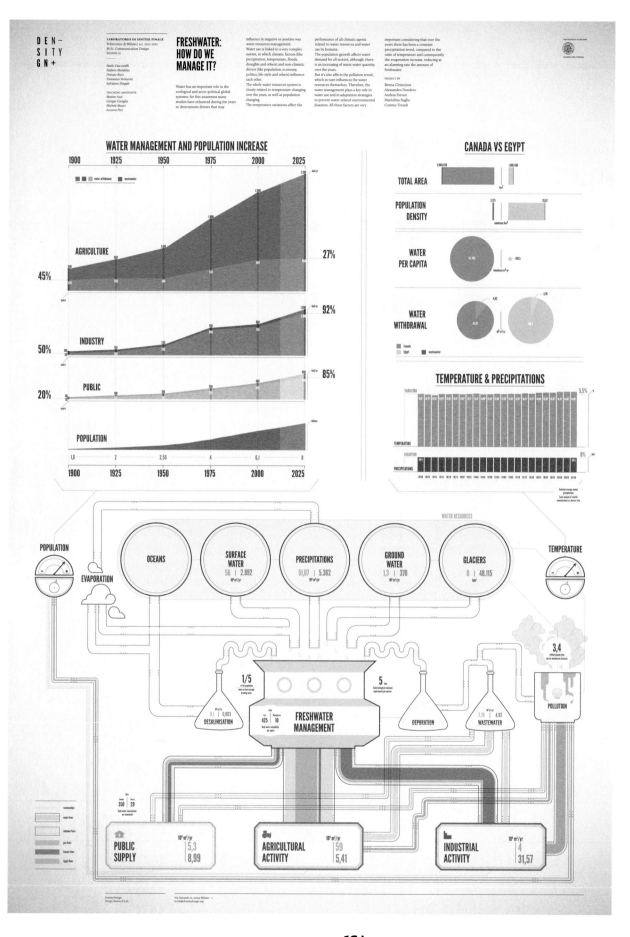

DEN—
SITY
GN+

LABORATORIO DI SINTESI FINALE
Politecnico di Milano | a.y. 2011-2012
M.Sc. Communication Design
Section c3

Paolo Ciuccarelli
Stefano Mandato
Donato Ricci
Tommaso Venturini
Salvatore Zingale

TEACHING ASSISTANTS
Matteo Azzi
Giorgio Caviglia
Michele Mauri
Azzurra Pini

PROJECT BY
Bruna Cirincione
Alessandro Dondero
Andrea Ferrari
Mariolina Suglia
Cosimo Torsoli

FRESHWATER: HOW DO WE MANAGE IT?

Water has an important role in the ecological and socio-political global systems; for this awareness many studies have enhanced during the years to determinate drivers that may influence in negative or positive way water resources management.
Water use is linked to a very complex system, in which climatic factors (like precipitation, temperature, floods, droughts and others) and non-climatic drivers (like population, economy, politics, life-style and others) influence each other.
The whole water resources system is closely related to temperature changing over the years, as well as population changing.
The temperature variations affect the performance of all climatic agents related to water resources and water use by humans.
The population growth affects water demand for all sectors, although, there is an increasing of waste water quantity over the years.
But it's also affects the pollution trend, which in turn influences the water resources themselves. Therefore, the water management plays a key role in water use and in adaptation strategies to prevent water-related environmental disasters. All these factors are very important considering that over the years there has been a constant precipitation trend, compared to the raise of temperature and consequently the evaporation increase, reducing at an alarming rate the amount of freshwater.

WATER MANAGEMENT AND POPULATION INCREASE

AGRICULTURE — 45% / 27%

INDUSTRY — 50% / 92%

PUBLIC — 20% / 85%

POPULATION

CANADA VS EGYPT

TOTAL AREA
POPULATION DENSITY
WATER PER CAPITA
WATER WITHDRAWAL

Canada
Egypt
wastewater

TEMPERATURE & PRECIPITATIONS

VARIATION — 5,5%
TEMPERATURE
VARIATION — 0%
PRECIPITATIONS

WATER RESOURCES

POPULATION
EVAPORATION
TEMPERATURE

OCEANS
SURFACE WATER — 56 | 2.892
PRECIPITATIONS — 51,07 | 5.362
GROUND WATER — 1,3 | 370
GLACIERS — 0 | 48.115

DESALINISATION — 0,1 | 0,003

1/5
of the population does not have enough drinking water

FRESHWATER MANAGEMENT
425 | 10

5 liter
daily biological minimum requirement per person

DEPURATION

WASTEWATER — 3,76 | 4,82

POLLUTION

3,4
million people/year die for waterborne diseases

PUBLIC SUPPLY — 5,3 / 8,99
350 | 20

AGRICULTURAL ACTIVITY — 59 / 5,41

INDUSTRIAL ACTIVITY — 4 / 31,57

by: DensityDesign //
   Bruna Cirincione, Alessandro
   Dondero, Andrea Ferrari,
   Mariolina Suglia, Cosimo Torsoli

in: Milan, Italy

Water plays an important role in the ecological and sociopolitical global systems. Its use is linked to a very complex system in which climatic factors (like precipitation, temperature, floods, droughts, and others) and non-climatic drivers (like population, economy, politics, lifestyle. and others) influence each other. A large number of studies explore the issue of water resources management and its correlations. So does the infographic **FRESHWATER: HOW DO WE MANAGE IT?** by DensityDesign, an interdisciplinary research lab dedicated to the visual representation of complex social, organizational, and urban phenomena. True to their mission of exploiting the potential of information design and providing innovative and engaging visual artifacts to enable researchers and scholars to build solid arguments, **FRESHWATER: HOW DO WE MANAGE IT?** gathers facts and figures, such as the alarming decrease of freshwater, rendering the necessity to use water responsibly in an accessible, visually engaging way.

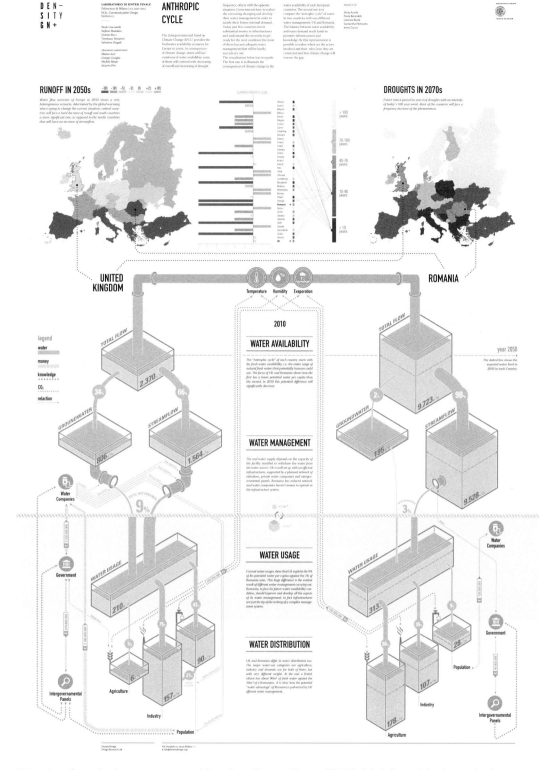

ANTHROPIC CYCLE

by: DensityDesign //
   Silvia Acerbi, Paola Berardelli,
   Lorenzo Berte', Samantha
   Pietrovito, Irene Zocco

in: Milan, Italy

Using data from the Intergovernmental Panel on Climate Change (IPCC), this infographic shows the future availability of fresh water in Europe, which will vary from too much to too little due to climate change. The data makes it clear that governments need to begin building better water management systems to deal with these issues, but only a few currently invest substantial money in these infrastructures. The second part of the infographic compares the water management systems of the United Kingdom and Romania using projected water levels for 2050. Despite having less water overall, the United Kingdom will have more water available to its citizens because of its efficient water management system.

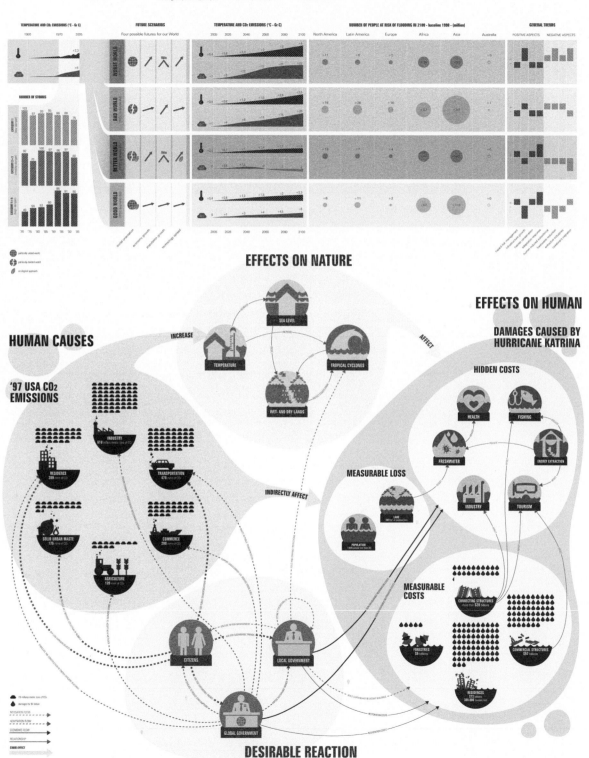

COULDA, WOULDA, SHOULDA
opposite page

by: DensityDesign //
Stefania Guerra, Michela Lazzaroni, Roberto Scotti, Ilaria Segreto, Jlenia Vertemara

in: Milan, Italy

Global warming is one the most urgent problems of our time. DensityDesign visualized the issue, focusing on particularly endangered areas such as coastal and low-lying regions. Having researched the present situation, possible scenarios, rising human-induced pressures on the environment, major causes of global warming, and inevitable consequences like erosion and floods, the research lab illustrated the "machinery" of climate change from the point of view of coastal systems. Incorporated into the graphic is existing data documenting the disastrous consequences caused by Hurricane Katrina that struck New Orleans's coasts in 2005. Presented in combination with North America's pollution data, it serves as a vivid and shocking reminder of what climate change has led to and is likely to lead to in the future. The graphic's "reaction" area gathers some good pieces of advice, indicating how both people and governments could slow down the process of global warming. Aiming to promote sustainability awareness and potential new laws, DensityDesign calls on everyone to act now.

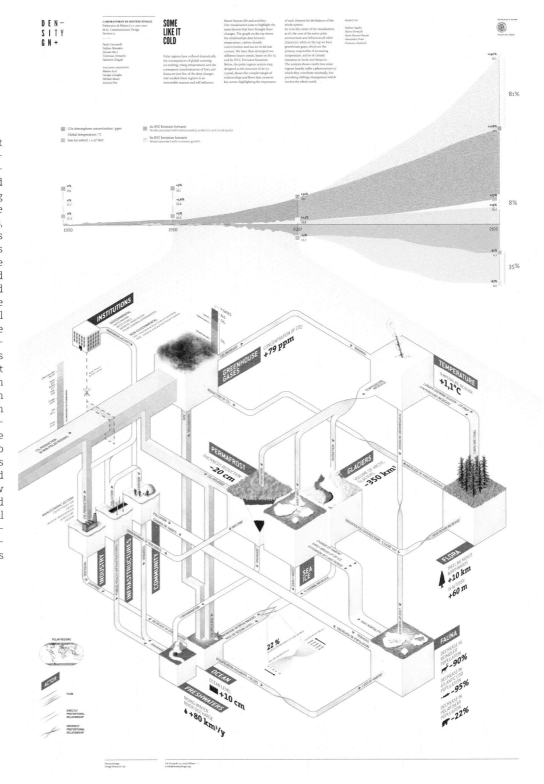

SOME LIKE IT COLD

by: DensityDesign //
Stefano Agabio, Marco Bernardi, Paolo Panzuti Bisanti, Alessandro Pomè, Francesco Pontiroli

in: Milan, Italy

Directly exposed to ice melting, rising temperatures, and the consequent transformation of flora and fauna, polar regions are particularly marked by the dramatic consequences of global warming. Working with the Final Synthesis Design Studio A.Y. and the MSc Communication Design Faculty of Design Politecnico di Milano, DensityDesign developed the visualization **SOME LIKE IT COLD**, aiming to highlight the main factors that cause climate change. The central part of the diagram is the "polar regions system map." Designed to resemble the structure of an ice crystal, it illustrates the complex tangle of relationships and causal chains, and draws attention to the importance of each element for the balance of the whole system.

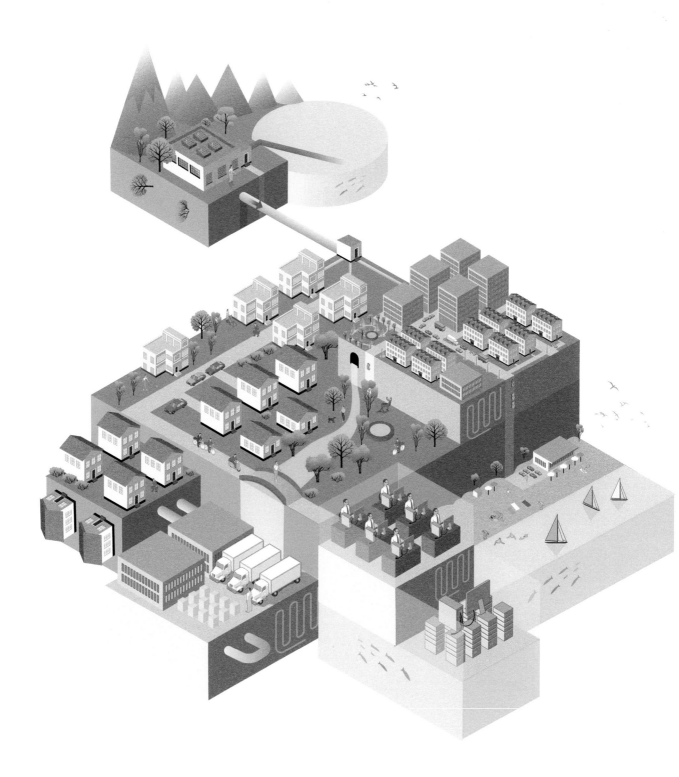

COOLING, HEATING

by: **Børge Bredenbekk,**
    VJU

for: Lyse

in: Norway

Lyse is one of the biggest suppliers of electricity and communication services on the west coast of Norway. In collaboration with VJU, Børge Bredenbekk created technical illustrations to explain the source and flow of the electricity, cooling, heating, and gas supplied by the company. The illustrations, which appeared in catalogs and online, explain the complex relationships these sources have to the system as a whole.

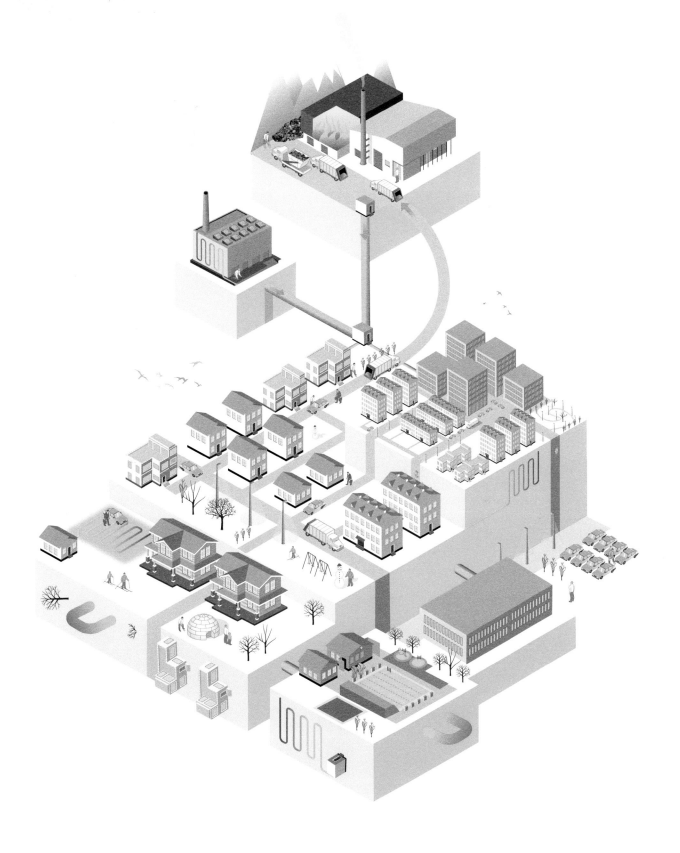

DEFORESTATION IN BRAZIL

by: Buraco de Bala //
    Aleixo Leite,
    Bruno Rojas,
    Emerson Rodrigues
for: WWF
in: Brasília, Brazil

DEFORESTATION is the third spot in the World Wildlife Fund's series about human impact on the environment. It raises awareness of Brazil's biggest problem when it comes to global warming and environmental destruction: deforestation. Animation studio Buraco de Bala used an animated series of infographics to reveal just how much urban dwellers rely on the well-being of their forests. This 30-second spot uses a playful animation style to get its sobering message across succinctly and with a touch of humor.

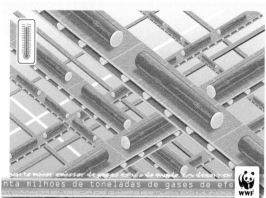

LES EKOVORES ^{opposite page}

by: FALTAZI //
    Laurent Lebot, Victor Massip
in: Nantes, France

Industrial designers Laurent Lebot and Victor Massip created LES EKOVORES as a solution to the causes of global warming. Their project is the blueprint for a modern urban utopia, in which consumers and food and energy producers live in sustainable symbiosis. The illustration of the system is a bird's-eye view of an urban community where daily needs are met through a balance of urban districts and agricultural sectors in close proximity to one another. Public facilities, farms, local business, and private homes would operate in a closed loop with short supply channels to minimize the need for fossil fuels. The resulting infrastructure of independent farm districts, local food supplies, and recycled waste plants would create sustainable economies and communities.

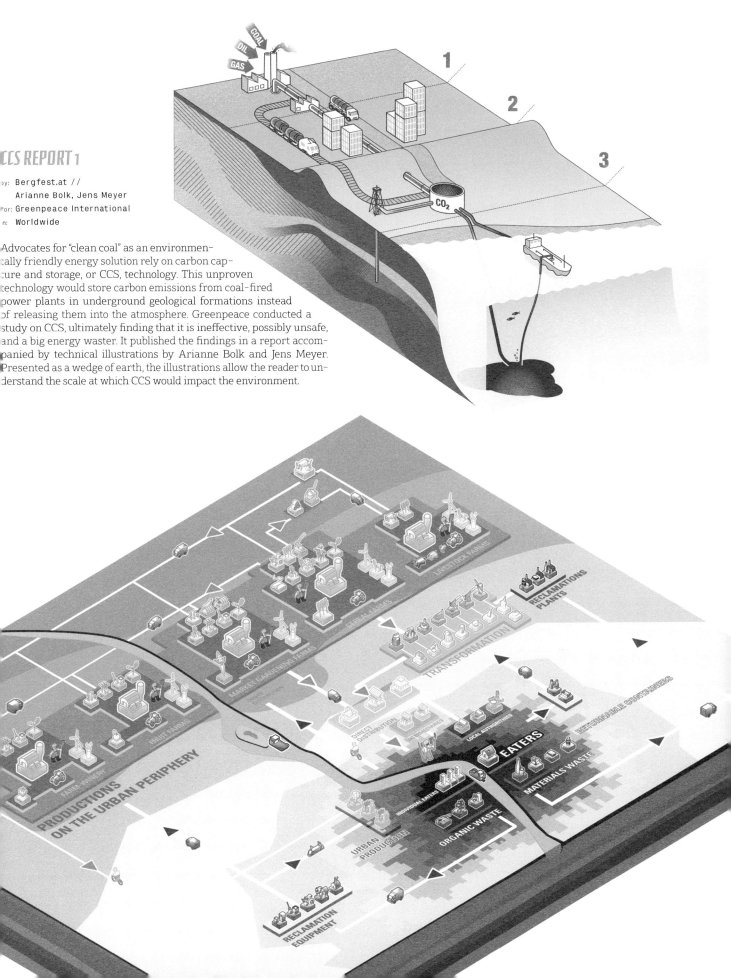

CCS REPORT 1

by: Bergfest.at //
Arianne Bolk, Jens Meyer
for: Greenpeace International
in: Worldwide

Advocates for "clean coal" as an environmentally friendly energy solution rely on carbon capture and storage, or CCS, technology. This unproven technology would store carbon emissions from coal-fired power plants in underground geological formations instead of releasing them into the atmosphere. Greenpeace conducted a study on CCS, ultimately finding that it is ineffective, possibly unsafe, and a big energy waster. It published the findings in a report accompanied by technical illustrations by Arianne Bolk and Jens Meyer. Presented as a wedge of earth, the illustrations allow the reader to understand the scale at which CCS would impact the environment.

ECOCHALLENGE

by: Raureif, Berlin //
   Timm Kekeritz
for: University of Applied
   Sciences Potsdam
in: Berlin, Germany

ECOCHALLENGE is an iPhone app that supports ecologically responsible living. Developed as part of the "EcoViz" research program at the University of Applied Sciences Potsdam, it sets playful little challenges that aid everyone to live sustainably. Interactive calculators, educational infographics and weekly updates supply additional information and help develop a better understanding for ecological matters. Sleek, contemporary graphics promote sustainability as an essentially cool modern-day must. A social component allows users to compete with their friends through Facebook, adding a competitive streak to the sustainability challenge.

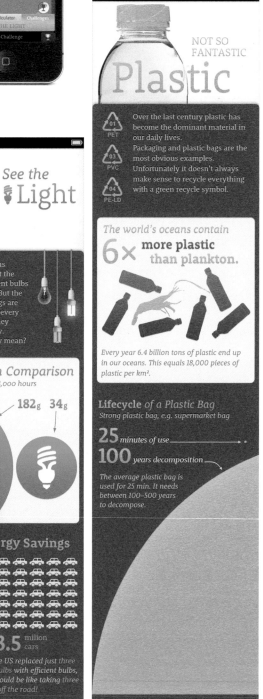

VIRTUAL WATER

by: Raureif, Berlin //
   Timm Kekeritz
for: University of Applied
   Sciences Potsdam
in: Berlin, Germany

A surprising number of products like coconuts, cheese, and chocolate have high water footprints. The VIRTUAL WATER project aims to educate consumers on these hidden water footprints in the hopes that they will rethink their consumption patterns. Designer Timm Kekeritz created a poster that uses infographics to explain how much water it takes to produce common products like one bottle of beer, a pound of potatoes, or a cotton T-shirt. In addition to the poster, the VIRTUAL WATER smartphone app allows users to compare products and adjust product amounts

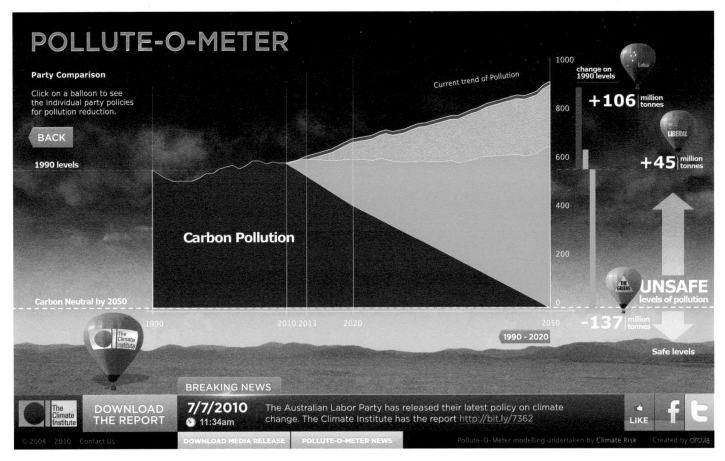

THE POLLUTE-O-METER

by: circul8 //
     Jamie Madden, Michael Ashton
for: The Climate Institute
in: Sydney, Australia

THE POLLUTE-O-METER is an interactive Web graphic that takes the environmental policies of the three major Australian political parties and projects them 40 years into the future. Commissioned by the Climate Institute before the 2010 election, data from the Greens, Liberal, and Labour parties were converted into an infographic with hot-air balloons representing each party. The statistics, which update in real time, allow voters to analyze fresh information and force politicians to be accountable for their policies. Direct links to social media sites allow the user to easily share the information with others.

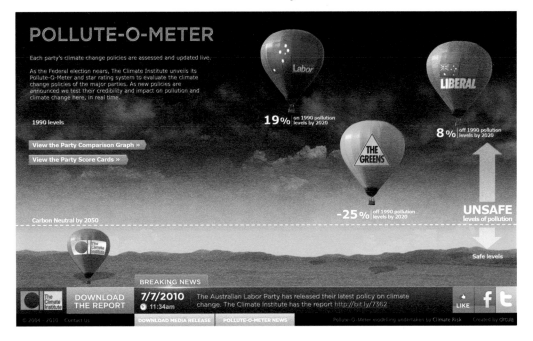

TRINKWASSERGEWINNUNG PRO JAHR

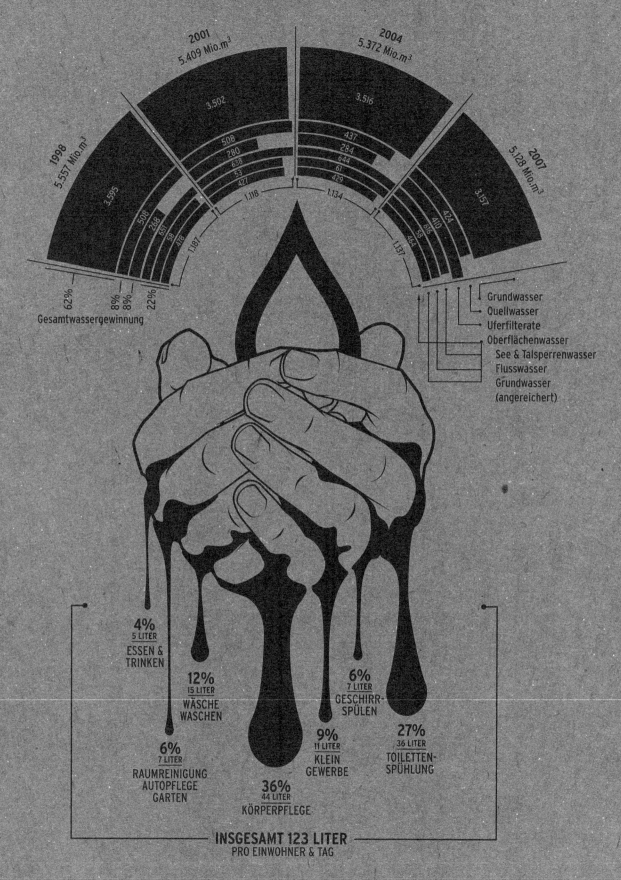

2001
5.409 Mio.m³

2004
5.372 Mio.m³

1998
5.557 Mio.m³

2007
5.128 Mio.m³

3.502

3.595

3.516

3.157

508
280
638
53
427
1.118

508
268
651
58
478
1.187

437
284
644
61
429
1.134

424
410
596
56
464
1.137

62%   8% 8% 22%

Gesamtwassergewinnung

Grundwasser
Quellwasser
Uferfilterate
Oberflächenwasser
See & Talsperrenwasser
Flusswasser
Grundwasser
(angereichert)

4%
5 LITER
ESSEN &
TRINKEN

12%
15 LITER
WÄSCHE
WASCHEN

6%
7 LITER
RAUMREINIGUNG
AUTOPFLEGE
GARTEN

36%
44 LITER
KÖRPERPFLEGE

9%
11 LITER
KLEIN
GEWERBE

6%
7 LITER
GESCHIRR-
SPÜLEN

27%
36 LITER
TOILETTEN-
SPÜHLUNG

INSGESAMT 123 LITER
PRO EINWOHNER & TAG

TRINKWASSERVERWENDUNG IM HAUSHALT
IN DEUTSCHLAND (2010) PRO KOPF/TAG

Quelle: Bundesverband der Energie- und Wasserwirtschaft e. V.

WASSERGEWINNUNG ^{opposite page}

by: greatmade //
typism
for: design.idee
in: Erfurt, Germany

An infographic about drinking water production and usage in Germany. Data from 1998 to 2010 was sampled and broken down, showing that the majority of Germany's water supply comes from groundwater. Each day, citizens use half of that water for bathing and flushing inefficient toilets. By making people aware of where water is being used, they can adjust their daily habits and help conserve the water supply.

MY WATER DIARY

by: DED Associates //
Jon Daughtry,
Rob Barber
for: Free Radicals
in: Sheffield, U.K.

Presented by Free Radicals, a growing group of academics across four universities that work with experienced professionals from various fields on sustainable solutions to key world problems, the iPhone app MY WATER DIARY allows customers to track their water usage over a week. Part of the "Water Amnesty" project, the App supports responsible consumption by creating a sense of used quantities and of water as a precious and finite resource that is likely to become scarcer in the future.

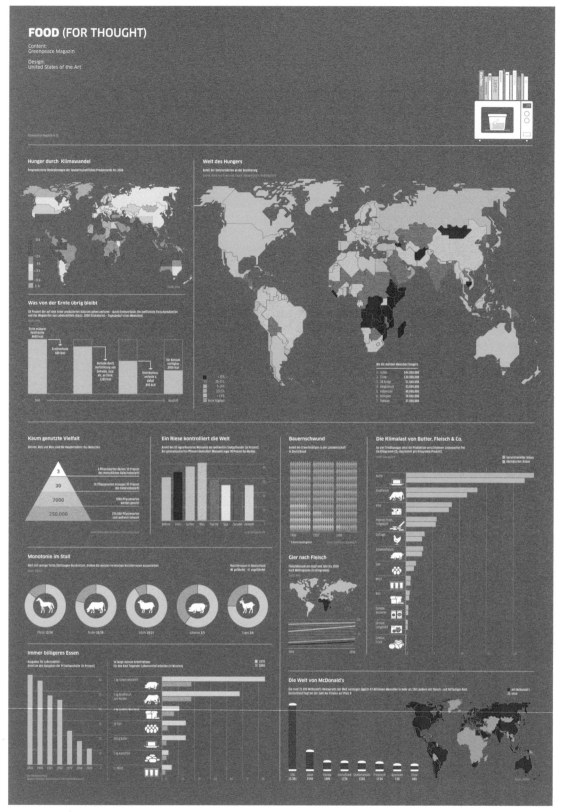

FOOD (FOR THOUGHT)

by: United States of the Art //
Carsten Raffel
for: greenpeace magazin
in: Hamburg, Germany

The April 2010 issue of *greenpeace magazin* focused on the theme of food. This infographic about agriculture and sustainability was created for the issue and subsequently turned into a poster. Although it condenses a large amount of information onto one page, the presentation is kept fresh and clear by using a variety of graphs, maps, tables, and charts to illustrate topics such as how many minutes an employee must work to buy food products, the lack of diversity in the human diet, and percentages of food wasted because of inefficient harvesting practices. The information is framed in historical and geographic contexts, helping the reader understand the way food production and consumption has changed based on a variety of global factors.

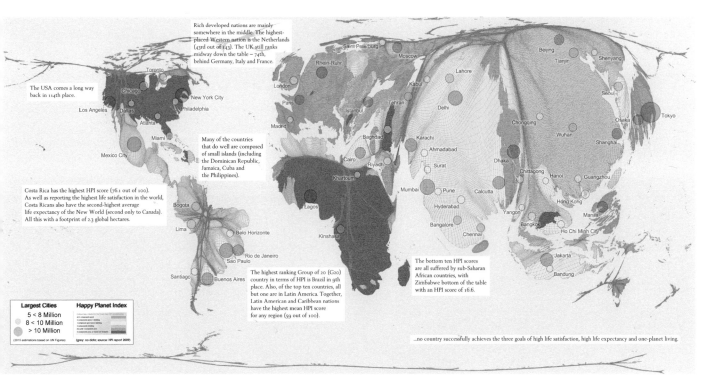

Rich developed nations are mainly somewhere in the middle. The highest-placed Western nation is the Netherlands (43rd out of 143). The UK still ranks midway down the table – 74th, behind Germany, Italy and France.

The USA comes a long way back in 114th place.

Many of the countries that do well are composed of small islands (including the Dominican Republic, Jamaica, Cuba and the Philippines).

Costa Rica has the highest HPI score (76.1 out of 100). As well as reporting the highest life satisfaction in the world, Costa Ricans also have the second-highest average life expectancy of the New World (second only to Canada). All this with a footprint of 2.3 global hectares.

The highest ranking Group of 20 (G20) country in terms of HPI is Brazil in 9th place. Also, of the top ten countries, all but one are in Latin America. Together, Latin American and Caribbean nations have the highest mean HPI score for any region (59 out of 100).

The bottom ten HPI scores are all suffered by sub-Saharan African countries, with Zimbabwe bottom of the table with an HPI score of 16.6.

...no country successfully achieves the three goals of high life satisfaction, high life expectancy and one-planet living.

Largest Cities	Happy Planet Index
5 < 8 Million	
8 < 10 Million	
> 10 Million	

(2015 estimations based on UN Figures)   (grey: no data; source: HPI report 2009)

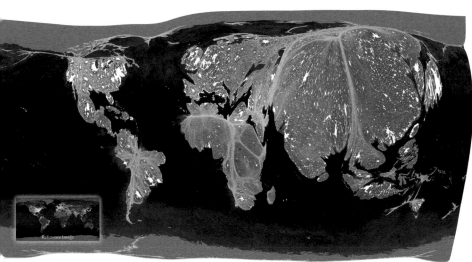

Reference Image

THE REAL EARTH AT NIGHT

by: University of Sheffield //
    Benjamin D. Hennig
for: The Leverhulme Trust
in: Sheffield, U.K.

THE REAL EARTH AT NIGHT is a new perspective on satellite images of the Earth at night. Light and dark areas on these images appear to show the world's socioeconomic disparities, but the true disparities become apparent when the image is re-projected onto a gridded world population cartogram. This gives every human being the same amount of space while retaining geographical references. In doing so, the planet's most populated places appear bigger, while the sparsely populated regions disappear from the map. The new map can be seen as the real Earth at night because it no longer gives the misleading impression that lights represent the most populated areas. The map was used in a lecture at the Royal Geographical Society about the environment and inequality.

MAPPING A (UN)HAPPY HUMANITY: A NEW PERSPECTIVE ON OUR PLANET'S WELL-BEING

by: University of Sheffield //
    Benjamin D. Hennig
for: the new economics foundation,
    Centre for Health and Well-being in
    Public Policy at the University of
    Sheffield
in: Sheffield, U.K.

The Happy Planet Index (HPI) was developed by the new economics foundation as an alternative method of mapping international standards of living. It focuses on the relationship of sustainability to quality of life by analyzing the resource consumption, life expectancy, life satisfaction, and ecological footprint of 143 countries. The gridded population projection used in the HPI map draws a more accurate picture of the (un)happy planet by putting population into perspective. This reveals the real efficiency with which nations convert the planet's natural resources into long and happy lives for their citizens.

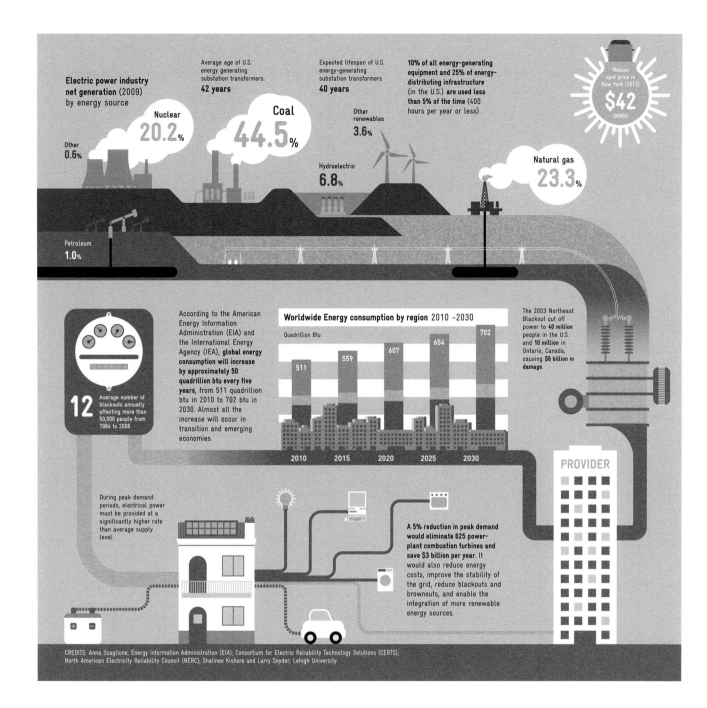

Electric power industry net generation (2009) by energy source

Nuclear **20.2**%

Coal **44.5**%

Other **0.6**%

Other renewables **3.6**%

Hydroelectric **6.8**%

Natural gas **23.3**%

Petroleum **1.0**%

Average age of U.S. energy generating substation transformers: **42 years**

Expected lifespan of U.S. energy-generating substation transformers **40 years**

10% of all energy-generating equipment and 25% of energy-distributing infrastructure (in the U.S.) **are used less than 5% of the time** (400 hours per year or less)

Median spot price in New York (2011) **$42** (MWh)

12 Average number of blackouts annually affecting more than 50,000 people from 1984 to 2006

According to the American Energy Information Administration (EIA) and the International Energy Agency (IEA), **global energy consumption will increase by approximately 50 quadrillion btu every five years**, from 511 quadrillion btu in 2010 to 702 btu in 2030. Almost all the increase will occur in transition and emerging economies.

Worldwide Energy consumption by region 2010 –2030

Quadrillion Btu

2010	2015	2020	2025	2030
511	559	607	654	702

The 2003 Northeast Blackout cut off power to **40 million** people in the U.S. and **10 million** in Ontario, Canada, causing **$6 billion in** damage.

During peak demand periods, electrical power must be provided at a significantly higher rate than average supply level.

A 5% reduction in peak demand would eliminate 625 power-plant combustion turbines and save $3 billion per year. It would also reduce energy costs, improve the stability of the grid, reduce blackouts and brownouts, and enable the integration of more renewable energy sources.

PROVIDER

CREDITS: Anna Scaglione; Energy Information Administration (EIA); Consortium for Electric Reliability Technology Solutions (CERTS); North American Electricity Reliability Council (NERC); Shalinee Kishore and Larry Snyder, Lehigh University

ELECTRICITY GRID IN THE U.S.

by: Infonauts // Carlos Coelho
for: Lehigh University
in: USA

Looking to illustrate the problems of the U. S. electricity grid in a visually attractive and engaging way that would appeal to their (former) students, Lehigh University commissioned Infonauts to translate a selection of relevant statistical information into graphics. Featured in the university's alumni magazine, the result showcases facts on energy consumption worldwide. To avoid stacks of bar graphs or other conventional forms of statistic representation, Infonauts developed a range of icons and illustrations. The result is a vivid, illustrated journey that shows the flow of electricity—from production, over transmission, to supply and end consumption.

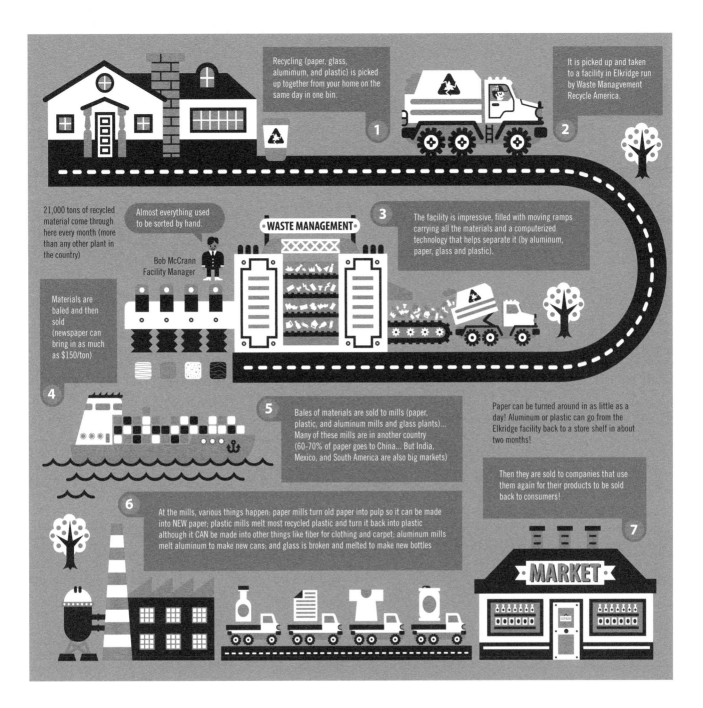

Recycling (paper, glass, alumimum, and plastic) is picked up together from your home on the same day in one bin.

1

It is picked up and taken to a facility in Elkridge run by Waste Managvement Recycle America.

2

21,000 tons of recycled material come through here every month (more than any other plant in the country)

Almost everything used to be sorted by hand.

Bob McCrann
Facility Manager

WASTE MANAGEMENT

3

The facility is impressive, filled with moving ramps carrying all the materials and a computerized technology that helps separate it (by aluminum, paper, glass and plastic).

Materials are baled and then sold (newspaper can bring in as much as $150/ton)

4

5

Bales of materials are sold to mills (paper, plastic, and aluminum mills and glass plants)... Many of these mills are in another country (60-70% of paper goes to China... But India, Mexico, and South America are also big markets)

Paper can be turned around in as little as a day! Aluminum or plastic can go from the Elkridge facility back to a store shelf in about two months!

Then they are sold to companies that use them again for their products to be sold back to consumers!

6

At the mills, various things happen: paper mills turn old paper into pulp so it can be made into NEW paper; plastic mills melt most recycled plastic and turn it back into plastic although it CAN be made into other things like fiber for clothing and carpet; aluminum mills melt aluminum to make new cans; and glass is broken and melted to make new bottles

MARKET

7

WASTE MANAGEMENT

by: Jan Kallwejt
for: Baltimore magazine
in: Baltimore, USA

The recycling company Waste Management Recycle America manages recyclable waste for the city of Baltimore. This infographic informs citizens about the actual process of recycling, taking them through the sorting and reuse timeline and providing facts about the modernization of the process, which has been sped up in recent years by automated systems. Making the recycling process more transparent for citizen recyclers encourages continued involvment—and hopefully gains new participants, too.

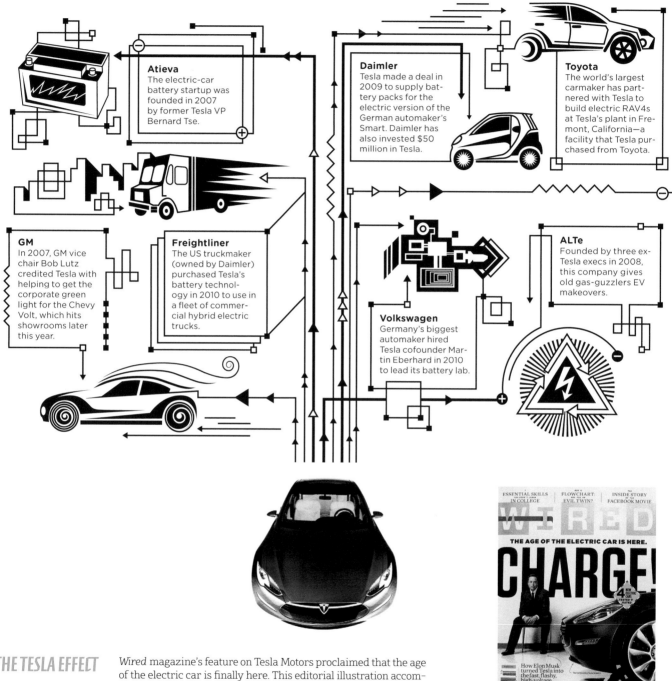

Atieva
The electric-car battery startup was founded in 2007 by former Tesla VP Bernard Tse.

Daimler
Tesla made a deal in 2009 to supply battery packs for the electric version of the German automaker's Smart. Daimler has also invested $50 million in Tesla.

Toyota
The world's largest carmaker has partnered with Tesla to build electric RAV4s at Tesla's plant in Fremont, California—a facility that Tesla purchased from Toyota.

GM
In 2007, GM vice chair Bob Lutz credited Tesla with helping to get the corporate green light for the Chevy Volt, which hits showrooms later this year.

Freightliner
The US truckmaker (owned by Daimler) purchased Tesla's battery technology in 2010 to use in a fleet of commercial hybrid electric trucks.

ALTe
Founded by three ex-Tesla execs in 2008, this company gives old gas-guzzlers EV makeovers.

Volkswagen
Germany's biggest automaker hired Tesla cofounder Martin Eberhard in 2010 to lead its battery lab.

THE TESLA EFFECT

by: MWM Graphics //
Matt W. Moore
for: WIRED MAGAZINE
in: Portland (Maine), USA

Wired magazine's feature on Tesla Motors proclaimed that the age of the electric car is finally here. This editorial illustration accompanied the story, which chronicled the growth of Tesla Motors and its influence on other companies in the automobile industry. The illustration by MWM Graphics highlights each of these relationships—from supplying battery packs to Daimler, to convincing the boardroom at GM to develop the Chevy Volt, to invigorating the auto industry to invest in green technology by paying other companies to manufacture its product. But most important has been its leadership in bringing the auto industry closer to phasing out the gasoline-powered car.

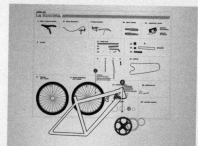

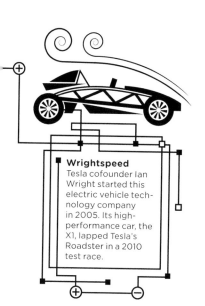

Wrightspeed
Tesla cofounder Ian Wright started this electric vehicle technology company in 2005. Its high-performance car, the X1, lapped Tesla's Roadster in a 2010 test race.

ARMAS PARA SALVAR EL PLANETA — LA BICICLETA

by: 3erMundo //
Ramón París,
Tere Castillo
for: Canal+
in: Barcelona,
Spain

The Spanish satellite broadcasting company Canal+ commissioned 3erMundo to create short spots for inclusion in a programming package dedicated to climate change. These graphic essays visually communicate the idea that we already have the tools we need to stop climate change. The four-part animated series, **ARMAS PARA SALVAR EL PLANETA** (Weapons to Save the Planet), energetically highlights the bicycle, the seed, the bee, and citizen X as affordable and accessible tools that can be put immediately to use to stop climate change.

VISUALIZING INDICATOR SYSTEMS USING THE EXAMPLE OF SUSTAINABLE DEVELOPMENT IN SWITZERLAND

by: Von B und C, Hahn und
Zimmermann //
Barbara Hahn, Christine
Zimmermann

for: Berne University of the Arts,
Swiss Federal Statistical Office,
Federal Office for Spatial Devel-
opment

in: Bern, Switzerland

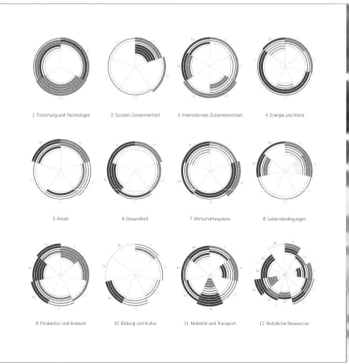

This research project developed alternative ways of visualizing data
for MONET, Switzerland's method
of measuring sustainable develop-
ment data. Instead of using pie charts or bar graphs, the project developed
three new visual systems called rhomb, typography, and circle visualiza-
tions. Aimed at their target audiences in the policy, administration, education and public relations/media sectors, they individually communicate
concepts of space, time, proportion, and quantity in a clearly comprehensible manner.

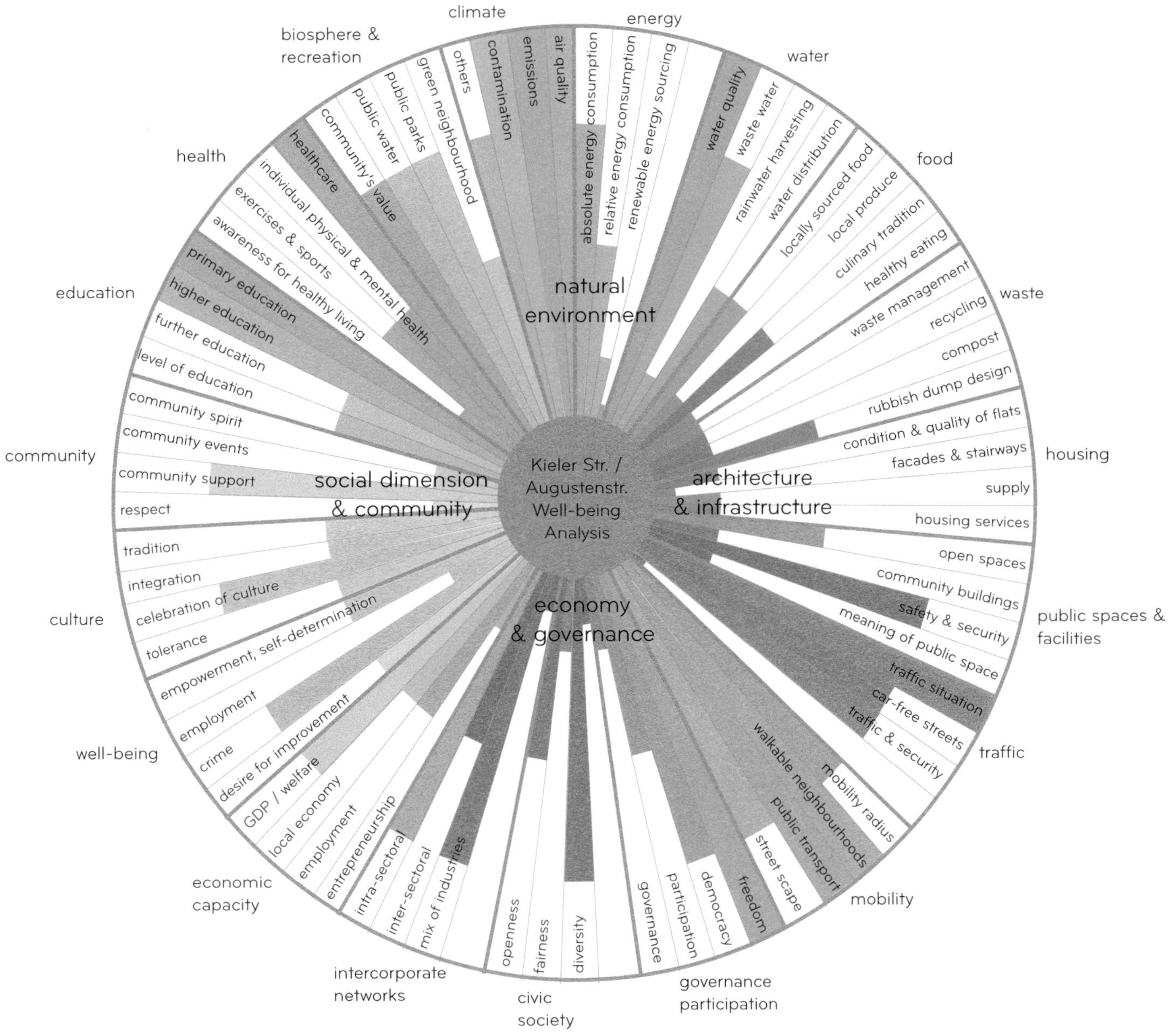

climate
energy
water
food
waste
housing
public spaces & facilities
traffic
mobility
governance participation
civic society
intercorporate networks
economic capacity
well-being
culture
community
education
health
biosphere & recreation
others
contamination
emissions
air quality
absolute energy consumption
relative energy consumption
renewable energy sourcing
water quality
waste water
rainwater harvesting
water distribution
locally sourced food
local produce
culinary tradition
healthy eating
waste management
recycling
compost
rubbish dump design
condition & quality of flats
facades & stairways
supply
housing services
open spaces
community buildings
safety & security
meaning of public space
traffic situation
car-free streets
traffic & security
mobility radius
walkable neighbourhoods
public transport
street scape
freedom
democracy
participation
governance
diversity
fairness
openness
mix of industries
inter-sectoral
intra-sectoral
entrepreneurship
employment
local economy
GDP / welfare
desire for improvement
crime
employment
empowerment, self-determination
tolerance
celebration of culture
integration
tradition
respect
community support
community events
community spirit
level of education
further education
higher education
primary education
awareness for healthy living
exercises & sports
individual physical & mental health
healthcare
community's value
public water
public parks
green neighbourhood
natural environment
architecture & infrastructure
economy & governance
social dimension & community
Kieler Str. / Augustenstr. Well-being Analysis

WELL-BEING WHEEL

by: Clear Village
for: Anglo-German Asset Management Company
in: Kiel, Germany

Clear Village explores new ways of harnessing content from statistical data and other research, and of translating it into the different "languages" spoken across the entire spectrum of stake-holders, ranging from local community groups to executive boardrooms. Commissioned by The Anglo-German Asset Management Company, they conducted the Well-Being Analysis in Gaarden-Ost, a neighborhood close to the German city of Kiel. Visualized as the **WELL-BEING WHEEL**, the analysis provides insight into key parameters of tenant satisfaction and dissatisfaction to enable landlords to improve overall tenant well-being. Although the analysis is supported by research, it is above all about reaching out to the community, engaging its members, and collating their feedback and views. In a larger context, the Well-Being Analysis sits between a proactive engagement device for getting a relatively intuitive status of the sustainability intelligence of a place and gross-national-happiness-type initiatives which aim to foster a framework for resilient life-quality improvements.

CHAPTER 3

BRAVE NEW WORLD

Design has the important task of accompanying the discourse on a required change of culture and values. Design will sensitize, convey, and assist in forging a new, constructive identity. The aesthetic dimension of sustainability plays a pivotal role in this process. We are today engaged in a competition between two models of civilization: on the one hand, our current consumer society that is attractive but not sustainable, and on the other, the vision of a culture of sustainability that must be at least as attractive and even more desirable in order to gain broad support in the population.[1]

Design is in a position to provide a projection screen for this vision. Yet this possibility has been neglected for much too long. In the German daily *Süddeutsche Zeitung*, Oliver Herwig once asked: "How much design can the good, the truth, and authenticity take?"[2] Of course, with the help of illusions design first contributed to creating a consumer culture that is based on wasting resources and destroying the environment. This is probably one of the reasons why design is often met with skepticism or mistrust in the context of sustainability instead of being grasped as an opportunity. Design must depart from creating ever-new, fashionable, one-day wonders. Sustainable design conveys conceptually shaped system solutions that communicate in an attractive and alluring language. Designer John Thackara writes: "In a less-stuff-more-people world, we still need systems, platforms, and services that enable people to interact more effectively and enjoyably. Sensitivity to context, to relationships, and to consequences are key aspects of the transition from mindless development to design mindfulness."[3] Sustainable design shapes contexts of use and action, and influences processes of life. It mediates

between consumers, the environment, and the economy. Companies that anchor credible sustainability in their corporate policy and consistently communicate this to their stakeholders and internally using visually extraordinary images possess a high differentiation potential on the market, as they are regarded as progressive in economic and ecological terms. Innovative enterprises and institutions utilize the potential of design strategies and images to make the complex processes of sustainable transformation comprehensible without pointing the finger. They gain social legitimacy and contribute to transforming society in a sustainable way.[4]

Many firms have long focused on sending cultural messages in order to secure the foundations of their market success with symbolic worlds. Sustainably manufactured clothes are beautiful, sustainable nutrition is enjoyable, the sustainable handling of mobility expresses quality of life—to create such

SUSTAINABLE DESIGN CONVEYS CONCEPTUALLY SHAPED SYSTEM SOLUTIONS THAT COMMUNICATE IN AN ATTRACTIVE AND ALLURING LANGUAGE.

combinations on the symbolic level is the big challenge for companies on the path to sustainable development.[5] On the following pages we present companies, institutions, products, and projects that employ cross-media campaigns and corporate design concepts that demonstrate in an exemplary way how this can function.

FOOTNOTES

1. See Glauber 2006
2. See Herwig 2011
3. See Thackara 2005
4. See Brugger 2008
5. See Pfriem 2006

LIST OF LITERATURE

Brugger, Florian (2008): Unternehmerische Nachhaltigkeitskommunikation, Lüneburg: Leuphana Universität Lüneburg

Glauber, Hans (Hg.) (2006): Langsamer Weniger Besser Schöner, München: oekom verlag

Herwig, Oliver (2011): Zu schön, um Bio zu sein, in http://www.sueddeutsche.de/leben/oeko-produkte-und-design-zu-schoen-um-bio-zu-sein-1.1064933 (letzter Zugriff: 4.5.2012)

Pfriem, Reinhard (2006): Bleibt alles anders?, in Hans Glauber, (Hrsg.) 2006: Langsamer, weniger, besser, schöner, München: oekom verlag, 43)

Thackara, John (2005): In the bubble, Massachusetts: MIT Press

A positive attitude is the key to a happy life, for the planet and for us.

One Degree is all about you. There are tips and tools to reduce your own carbon footprint and incentives to make tackling climate change a priority every day. We will report on what we're doing, what impact we're having and how we can achieve more. One Degree of change.

Ask the people around you or check out the website.
1degree.net.au

One Degree
of attitude

by: Landor Associates //
Jason Little, Angela McCarthy,
Tim Warren, Mike Rigby, Steve Clarke
for: News Limited: One Degree
in: Sydney, Australia

In 2006, Rupert Murdoch challenged News Corporation and its associated businesses to become carbon neutral by 2010. The resulting campaign, **ONE DEGREE**, operates on a simple premise: the future of the planet can be altered if everyone changes their behavior by one degree. Instead of scaring employees into change, they were given information and practical tools to reduce their own carbon footprint. A feeling of community action was reinforced by using photographs and stories of people in the company. The campaign's logo further emphasized the power of the individual by combining the number and the degree symbol, which together represent a person.

Enlightening fact #1
Compact fluorescent lights pay for themselves within a year, last up to 10 times longer than conventional bulbs and save more than 66 per cent in lighting costs.

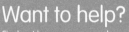

| WHAT WE ARE DOING | WHAT YOU CAN DO | LATEST NEWS | RESOURCES | CARBON CALCULATOR | STAFF |

Helping make things better by One Degree

Watch Rupert Murdoch's Climate Change Announcement

Want to help?
Find out how you can make a difference

News Limited Staff
Login

LEGAL | PRIVACY | WHAT WE ARE DOING | WHAT YOU CAN DO | LATEST NEWS | RESOURCES | CARBON CALCULATOR | STAFF

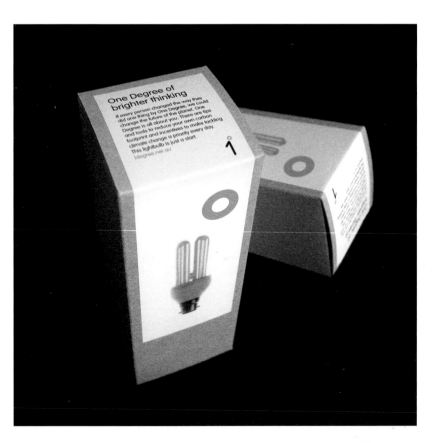

230,000L in one year
Each year the average
Australian household uses
230,000 litres of water.

WHAT WE ARE DOING · WHAT YOU CAN DO · LATEST NEWS · RESOURCES · CARBON CALCULATOR · STAFF

One Degree Home > What you can do

Energy

Recycling

Water

Lifestyle

LEGAL | PRIVACY | WHAT WE ARE DOING | WHAT YOU CAN DO | LATEST NEWS | RESOURCES | CARBON CALCULATOR | STAFF

How to offset your international flights.

WHAT WE ARE DOING · WHAT YOU CAN DO · LATEST NEWS · RESOURCES · CARBON CALCULATOR · STAFF

One Degree Home > What you can do > Energy

What you can do
Energy

Never mind nuclear power, wind power, clean coal, carbon trading and the rest. These may all have a role in preventing climate change in coming years but there's another, simpler way to tackle climate change.

It's estimated that worldwide, buildings account for about forty per cent of energy use, yet between a fifth and half of energy used in buildings is simply wasted through inefficiencies such as poor insulation or excess lighting.

That's a significant amount of greenhouse gas emissions, then, simply being pumped into the atmosphere for no good reason.

It also means we can make a real contribution to tackling climate change just by being smarter about the way we use energy in our homes and offices.

Once you start thinking about it, you can come up with hundreds of ways to save energy, many as simple as flicking a switch. And not only will it help prevent climate change, but

1 | 2 | 3

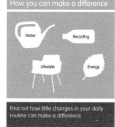

How you can make a difference

Water · Recycling · Lifestyle · Energy

Find out how little changes in your daily routine can make a difference

What does carbon neutral mean?

LEGAL | PRIVACY | WHAT WE ARE DOING | WHAT YOU CAN DO | LATEST NEWS | RESOURCES | CARBON CALCULATOR | STAFF

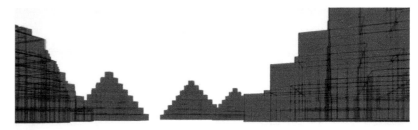

SHOEBOXES ACCOUNT FOR
MILLIONS OF TONS
OF WASTE.

We're **REDUCING** our
carbon dioxide by **10,000 tons**.

CLEVER
LITTLE BAG®

350734 01

Switching from our **RED SHOEBOX**
to **CLEVER LITTLE BAG**
will reduce our cardboard use by

65%

but may
one day
change the

BUSINESS **INDUSTRY**

This innovative system will save

8500 TONS of PAPER...

and
contribute
to a
better

world

BUSINESS INDUSTRY

CLEVER LITTLE BAG

by: fuseproject //
Yves Béhar
for: PUMA

PUMA manages to reconcile ecological responsibility with fashion consciousness like few other brands. Considering sustainability an essential part of contemporary lifestyle, it becomes a defining parameter for products and communications design. Under the motto "I'm half the bag I used to be," the shoe, sportswear, and lifestyle brand spreads the message along with some insightful facts and figures. Among many actions to reduce their carbon footprint is the use of smart packaging solutions. Bagging apparel collections in sustainable material, PUMA avoids 720 tons of polyethylene bags per year, which equals a saving of 29 million plastic bags — enough to cover an area the size of 1,000 football pitches. PUMA T-shirts are folded one more time to reduce the packaging size and thus save CO_2 emissions and costs during transport. Last but not least, they launched the PUMA **CLEVER LITTLE BAG**, a fashionable packaging system that eliminates the need for extra plastic carrier bags altogether. Conceived and designed with the aid of the creatives at fuseproject, the **CLEVER LITTLE BAG** soon came to be considered a highly desirable accessory. Installing recycling bins in their stores and outlets, PUMA encourages customers to return used shoes, clothing, and accessories of any brand to be recycled or properly disposed.

SWITCH TO CFLs & SAVE ENERGY.

If all New Yorkers switched to compact fluorescent lightbulbs, the energy savings could power the subways.

For more info & recycling locations visit nyc.gov/greenyc

TURN IT OFF.

Idling your engine contributes to asthma, cancer, & heart disease.

greeNYC

e
ENVIRONMENTAL
DEFENSE FUND

BIKE TO WORK DAY IS MAY 15.

GREENYC

by: HunterGatherer,
NYC & Company
for: GreeNYC
in: New York, USA

GREENYC is New York City's environmental initiative campaign. HunterGatherer was originally asked to develop a series of animations to accompany the mayor's launch of the campaign. Since then it has grown into a seasonal multimedia series, encompassing print, outdoor marketing, television, as well as retail partnerships and targeted mini-campaigns. The bird's simple and appealing messages convey environmental messages in a way that is friendly and approachable—and atypical of most green initiatives.

Bike to work. It's a zero carbon emission commute.

Join us from 7-10:30am for a snack at these locations:

City Hall Park
Queensboro Bridge, Queens Side
Williamsburg Bridge, Brooklyn Side
Manhattan Bridge, Manhattan Side
Brooklyn Bridge, Tower on Brooklyn Side
Madison Square Park

For information on over 200 events,
go to bikemonthnyc.org or call 311.

greeNYC

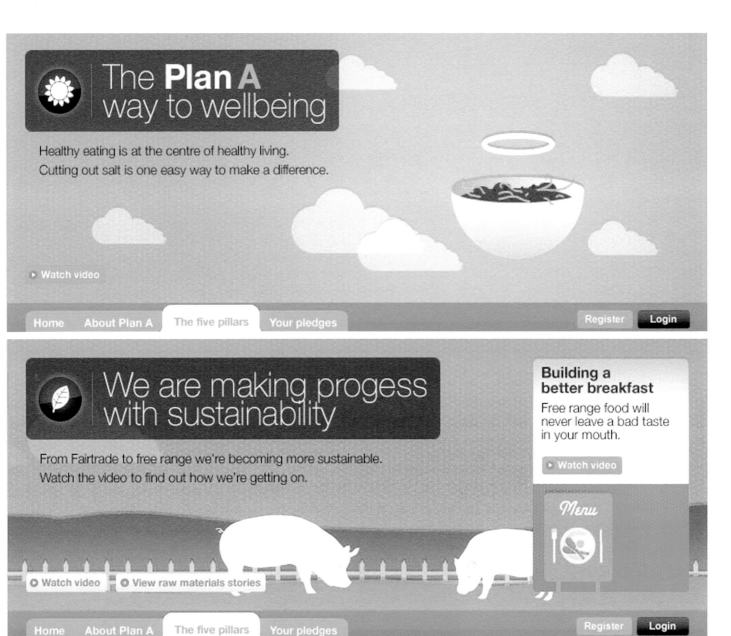

The **Plan A** way to wellbeing

Healthy eating is at the centre of healthy living.
Cutting out salt is one easy way to make a difference.

▶ Watch video

Home | About Plan A | The five pillars | Your pledges | Register | Login

We are making progess with sustainability

From Fairtrade to free range we're becoming more sustainable.
Watch the video to find out how we're getting on.

Building a better breakfast
Free range food will never leave a bad taste in your mouth.

▶ Watch video

Menu

⊙ Watch video | ⊙ View raw materials stories

Home | About Plan A | The five pillars | Your pledges | Register | Login

We are making progess to cut waste

Since we started charging for our food carrier bags we have seen an 80% reduction in the number of bags we've given out. Watch the video to find out how we're getting on.

The Plan A way to cut waste
Find out how our new 5p charge for carrier bags is helping.

▶ Watch video

⊙ Watch video | ⊙ View waste stories

Home | About Plan A | The five pillars | Your pledges | Register | Login

MARKS & SPENCER PLAN A WEBSITE

by: **Digit //**
    Bradley Cho-Smith
for: **Marks & Spencer**
in: **London, U.K.**

The **PLAN A WEBSITE** is the center of Marks & Spencer's initiative to complete 180 environmental commitments by the year 2015. It serves as a resource for ideas and progress updates, and as a place for customers to become involved in the project. Photographs, animations, and statistics present a wide variety of projects and goals for consumers to engage with, ensuring that everyone who wants to be participate can find a cause that suits them.

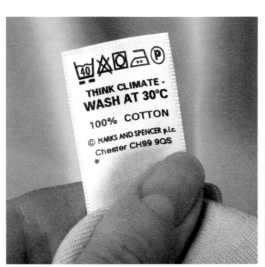

PLAN A

by: Marks & Spencer
for: Marks & Spencer Plan A
in: U.K.

Marks & Spencer created **PLAN A** as a collection of 180 commitments to achieve by the year 2015, with the ultimate goal of becoming the world's most sustainable major retailer. Working with their customers and suppliers to combat climate change, they are using the initiative to reduce waste, use sustainable raw materials, trade ethically, and help their customers to lead healthier lifestyles. Employees and customers are encouraged to participate in campaigns like "Forever Fish," which works with the Marine Conservation Society to clean up beaches. This not only gets Marks & Spencer closer to its goal, but helps strengthen communities, raise awareness, and benefit the environment.

CAMPAIGN NULL GRAD PLUS

by: Designliga—Büro für Visuelle
   Kommunikation und Innenarchitektur
for: Green City
in: Munich, Germany

As Europe's largest local environmental protection association, Green City focuses on climate, energy, mobility, and city planning and design. Designliga developed the branding for its NULL GRAD PLUS campaign in partnership with the marketing consultancy company Feld M. The campaign's serious message of ending practices that contribute to climate change is balanced out by the light voice of the branding, which invites citizens to change their behavior using a positive and engaging tone with playful illustrations. The use of the speech bubble as part of the NULL GRAD PLUS logo is repeated in its guerilla marketing campaign, which placed speech bubbles with various environmental messages throughout urban environments.

SCHONEN SIE IHR AUTO · ESSEN SIE WENIGER FLEISCH · NUTZEN SIE ENERGIESPARLAMPEN · ACHTEN SIE AUF IHREN STROMVERBRAUCH · WERDEN SIE AKTIV

STELLEN SIE UM AUF ÖKOSTROM · SCHALTEN SIE DIE STROMFRESSER AB · FLIEGEN SIE WENIGER · KAUFEN SIE LOKALE PRODUKTE · DUSCHEN SIE MAL WIEDER

STOPPEN WIR
DIE ERDERWÄRMUNG.

137

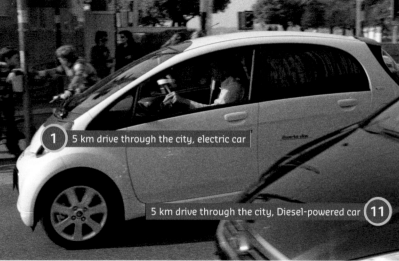

1 — 5 km drive through the city, electric car

5 km drive through the city, Diesel-powered car — 11

220 — flip flops, lifespan: 1 summer

324 — leather shoes, lifespan: 5 years

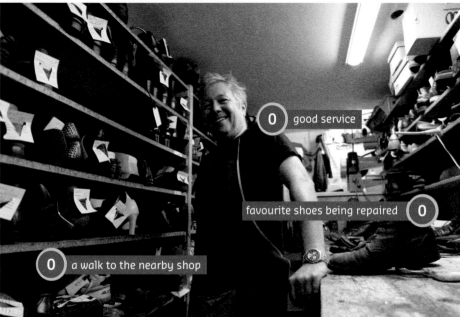

0 — good service

favourite shoes being repaired — 0

0 — a walk to the nearby shop

---

www.eingutertag.org

Ein guter Tag hat **100** Punkte.

Um unsere Welt und unser Klima im Gleichgewicht zu halten, müssen wir den Ausstoß an CO_2 deutlich reduzieren. Eine Menge von 6,8 kg davon darf jeder Mensch jeden Tag ausstoßen. Wir rechnen das um in 100 Punkte. Jeder Mensch hat jeden Tag 100 Punkte zur Verfügung. In Vorarlberg verbrauchen wir im Durchschnitt derzeit über 450 Punkte. Wir leben über unsere Verhältnisse.

6

5km Moped fahren

+

3

1 Flasche Mineralwasser

+

25

1 Hamburger

=

34

Prüfe, wie viele Punkte du im Alltag verbrauchst!

Fast jede Tätigkeit ist mit CO_2-Ausstoß verbunden. Die Heizung der Wohnung, die Milch zum Frühstück, die Fahrt zur Schule, das Schnitzel zu Mittag, die Stunden vor dem Computer …

Du hast die Wahl: Je weniger Punkte ein Produkt hat, desto besser. Je weniger Überflüssiges du konsumierst, desto besser.

50km travel by train — 15

 50km drive by car — 75

 50km ride by bicycle — 0

 500g grapes from South Africa — 40

500g organic apples — 1 BIO

500g organic bananas — 7 BIO

 200g fresh fish — 7

 1 tin of tuna — 28

 1L tap water — 0

 1L mineral water — 2

 4 cups of coffee — 4

 4 cups of tea — 1

 Coke, 330 ml PET bottle — 4

 1L apple juice — 4

 200g greenhouse tomatoes — 4

 200g organic tomatoes — 0.5 BIO

 1 role toilet paper — 4

 1 role toilet paper recycling material — 1

 1 hour watching TV — 1

 1 newspaper — 3

 1 T-shirt organic cotton — 10 BIO

 1 T-shirt — 80

 10 eggs — 30

 10 organic eggs — 15 BIO

 500g bread — 5

 100g cheese — 14

 1 pair of flip-flops — 220

  1 pair of leather shoes — 300

1L milk — 17

1L organic milk — 15 BIO

 1 cheeseburger — 35

200g pork — 12

 200g chicken — 10

     1 bar of chocolate — 5

A better day the 100 way.

15 lbs of CO_2 (100 points) is the amount each of us may emit on a daily basis by how they live, in order to keep our climate in balance. How much emission (points) relates to different goods or activities and what interesting alternatives are there? www.better-day.org

EIN GUTER TAG HAT 100 PUNKTE

by: Kairos, Integral Ruedi Baur //
Ruedi Baur, Christoph Breuer,
Axel Steinberger, Martin Strele,
Jana Strozinsky

in: Austria, Germany, Switzerland

The project **EIN GUTER TAG HAT 100 PUNKTE** (A Good Day Has 100 Points) challenges participants to calculate their contribution to CO_2 emissions—and ultimately reduce that number to a sustainable 100 points (6.8 kilograms). The project's interactive website, eingutertag.org, hosts a database of products and activities, each with an assigned number of points relative to the amount of CO_2 it produces. A user's daily points can then be logged and tracked on his or her own page. The addition of a planned smartphone app in the future will also add to the everyday usability of the database. Turning the issue into an ongoing, interactive exercise helps the user to easily adjust habits and find alternatives.

register with **mo**

mount **mo tag**
to your bike

3 0 1
collect miles with **mo** vehicles

more miles
=
less money

MO — A FLEXIBLE MOBILITY SYSTEM FOR THE CITY OF TOMORROW

by: LUNAR Europe, Green City,
uwid //
Dirk Hessenbruch

for: mo-bility.com

in: Munich, Germany

Many people are happy to live without a car — if easy alternatives are available. MO is an urban mobility system — a single-source of flexible and affordable bikes, public transportation options, and cars. Using a smartphone app, members can easily locate the closest bike, car, or station. Members collect miles when they travel by bike or public transportation; the more miles they accumulate, the less they pay, which creates incentives for long-term change. Infographics and a film were developed to explain the system using clean blue graphics that can be found throughout MO's branding, making their stations and vehicles easy for members to spot.

DriveNow

DRIVENOW

by: KKLD*, Sixt, Millhaus
for: DriveNow
in: Munich, Berlin,
Düsseldorf, Germany

DRIVENOW is a stationless car-sharing program by BMWi, MINI, and SIXT. Having defined a business area for all participating cities, DRIVENOW has its vehicles parked over all this area to be reserved by DRIVENOW members using either the accompanying website, where a film, designed and produced by KKLD*, illustrates the concept in greater detail, or via the DRIVENOW smartphone app. Developed by Sixt, the mobile application enables everyone to register as a DRIVENOW member, view all available cars, reserve one with two clicks and get directions to find it in "augmented reality" mode. With the naked eye, DRIVENOW vehicles are pleasingly hard to spot. Countering the blatant advertising look of most other rental schemes, the black, inconspicuously branded cars fare well with understatement. Started in Munich, DRIVENOW is currently expanding to other cities throughout Europe.

BATTERY SWITCH STATION

y: Better Place //
    Shai Agassi, Barak Hershkovitz

Aiming to encourage people to switch to electric driving, Better Place provides a network and services that make an electric car affordable to buy and easy to use, providing drivers with charge spots, battery switch stations, and systems that optimize the driving experience and minimize environmental impact and cost. Their BATTERY SWITCH STATION allows for immediate range extension during long trips. As soon as a battery runs low, the in-car software Oscar, directs drivers to the closest BATTERY SWITCH STATION, where a robot switches a depleted battery for a full one in a matter of minutes. Considering user experience one of the primary differentiators that future consumers will care about, Better Place sets great store on advanced in-car software and telematics, both in terms of technology and design. Developed by the interface experts at Novia, a Switch Station Managing App provides clever remote control and driver assistance. A nod to the well-tried ess-is-more principle, the clean and reduced look renders high-tech accessible and sustainable lifestyle fashionable.

better place

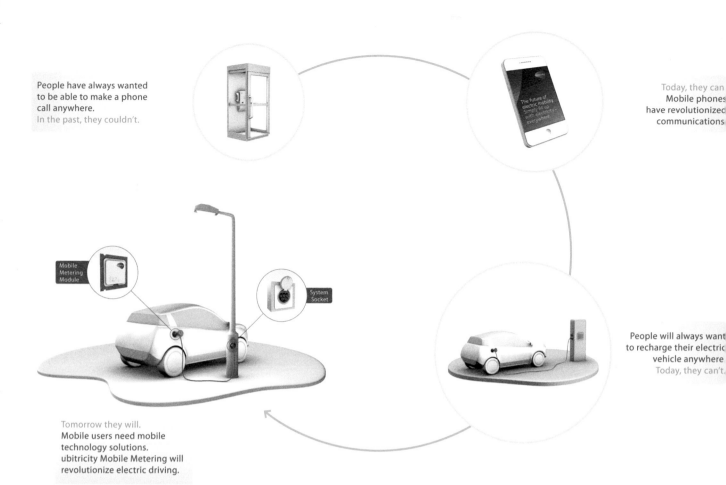

People have always wanted to be able to make a phone call anywhere.
In the past, they couldn't.

Today, they can
Mobile phones
have revolutionized
communications

People will always want
to recharge their electric
vehicle anywhere
Today, they can't.

Mobile
Metering
Module

System
Socket

Tomorrow they will.
Mobile users need mobile technology solutions.
ubitricity Mobile Metering will revolutionize electric driving.

UBITRICITY

by: plakken //
    Sebastian Stottele, Yves-Pierre Panzer
for: ubitricity
in: Berlin, Germany

The Berlin-based company **UBITRICITY** recognized that if electric cars are going to be widely used, a battery charging network must be widely available. They developed a solution that creates a dense but cost-effective battery charging network using mobile electronics as metering and billing units. Eliminating the expensive and rare conventional charging points clears the way for simple, cost-efficient system sockets, making the electric car more attractive and practical for drivers to use. Plakken developed ubitricity's website as well as advertising materials and a short film that explains how the system works and its advantages over other technologies.

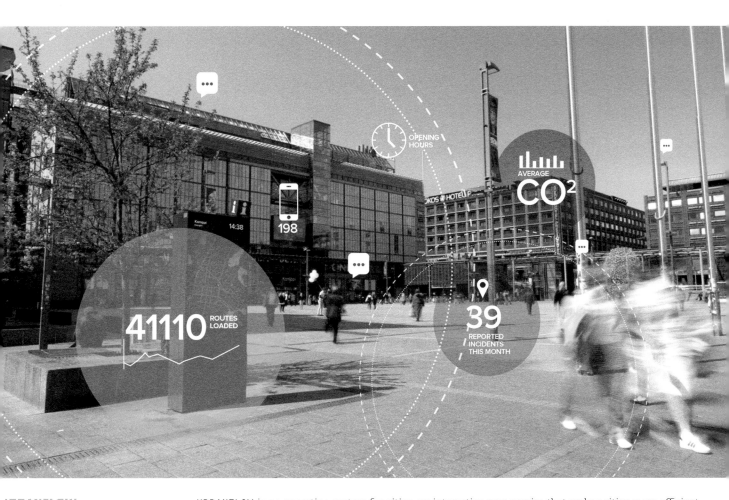

JRBANFLOW

y: Nordkapp //
   Sami Niemelä, Jukka Koops, Kate
   Whelan, Mayo Nissen, Akseli Anttila
τ: Helsinki, Finland

URBANFLOW is an operating system for cities, an interactive map service that makes cities more efficient and livable. The maps, available on screens installed throughout the city, combine ambient data such as traffic and air quality with public transportation schedules and bike paths for customized journey planning. The system can also calculate energy consumption numbers, CO_2 emissions, crime rates, and transportation statistics for more efficient city services that respond to environmental needs and citizen concerns. Nordkapp worked together with the urban design studio Urbanscale to develop the system's interface and concept video. Meticulously designed cartography, iconography, and language makes the data understandable and attractive.

145

BICYCLE COUNTER

by: Copenhagenize
    Consulting

for: ibikecph

in: Copenhagen,
   Denmark

The city of Copenhagen has become one of the most bicycle-friendly cities in the world. Its commitment to cycling as a major form of transportation has made it a role model for other cities hoping to increase bicycle traffic on their roads. One of their innovative ideas is an interactive digital bicycle counter installed on the City Hall Square, which sees 12,000 cyclists per day (12,000 on the other side of the street, too). Each time a cyclist passes, the counter is updated and displays the number for the cyclist to see. A sense of community is built by showing the cyclists their contribution to the larger whole, reinforcing the positive impact each cyclist has on the environment.

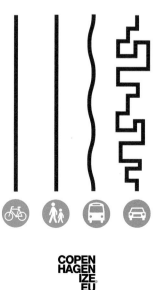

Copenhagenize Traffic Planning Guide

COPEN
HAGEN
IZE
EU

COPENHAGEN IN A BOX

by: Hello Monday
for: We are sailing
in: Denmark

This board game about Copenhagen is based on the classic real estate game, Monopoly. But in Hello Monday's version, environmentally sustainable choices are the way to win. Players move around the board with bicycle-shaped playing pieces, building Internet connections, parks, and wind turbines instead of erecting commercial properties. The game design relies on historical and contemporary events, photographs, and realistic money to introduce players to the city of Copenhagen and reinforce the message of sustainable urban planning and living.

147

Lass die
Sonne rein.

**DAUER
BRENNER**

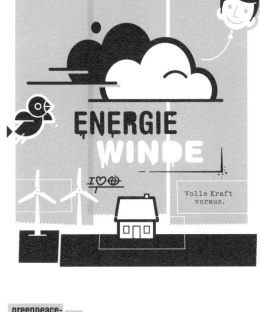

**ENERGIE
WINDE**

Volle Kraft
voraus.

Konsequenter
Ökostrom!

**DER UMWELT
ZULIEBE**

**SAUBERER
STROM**

Alles im Fluss.

STREET ART POSTAGE LABELS AND TOTE BAGS

by: United States of the Art //
     Carsten Raffel
for: Greenpeace Energy
in: Hamburg, Germany

Seven illustrations created for use on postage labels for the German post office and as tote bag graphics. Each illustration addresses either a climate-damaging energy source—such as coal, oil, and nuclear power—or a call to the greener, more sustainable energy practices of solar, wind, and hydro power. Printing the messages on stamps and bags brought them to a wider audience because they could be seen in private homes as well as in supermarkets, on public transportation, and on the street.

Grain
by grain

Bunch
by bunch

Scrub
by scrub

STEP BY STEP
SO MANY WAYS TO GO
FAIRTRADE

Every time you choose Fairtrade, farming
communities in the developing world take a step
away from poverty and towards a brighter future.

Take a step at fairtrade.org.uk/step

EVERY STEP COUNTS

Squeeze
by squeeze

Outfit
by outfit

Sip
by sip

Nibble
by nibble

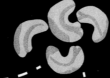

Scan here to make
your step count

PS5c

OR A **BIG & BOLD** ONE

MAKE IT A SMALL & SIMPLE **ONE**

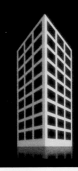

LIKE GETTING YOUR **OFFICE** TO DO IT TOO

LIKE SWAPPING YOUR USUAL TEA

LIKE GETTING YOUR **OFFICE** TO DO IT TOO

TO FAIRTRADE TEA

TAKE A STEP IN 2012

by: Lightmaker
for: The Fairtrade Foundation
in: U.K.

The Fairtrade Foundation's **TAKE A STEP** campaign calls on people in the United Kingdom to join the fight against an unfair trading system. Challenging the public to take a step in the right direction by thinking about what they can do every day, every week, or every month throughout 2012 to make a difference to the lives of farmers in the developing world, the campaign proposes a range of easy-to-realize actions: a first step could be someone buying their first packet of Fairtrade coffee, tea, or sugar; for someone further along the Fairtrade "journey," their step could be to find out if there is a "Fairtrade Town" campaign where they live; and for a seasoned Fairtrade campaigner, their step could be to organise a fun public event for Fairtrade Fortnight. Asking everyone who takes a step to register online, where steps will be displayed on an interactive "step-o-meter," the Fairtrade Foundation aims to take 1.5 million steps for Fairtrade in 2012. Seeking to appeal to the broad range of audiences and to reinforce their online presence, the foundation commissioned Lightmaker to develop a new microsite for the campaign, one that would create a sense of community and dialogue with prominent calls to action and outbound links to social media channels.

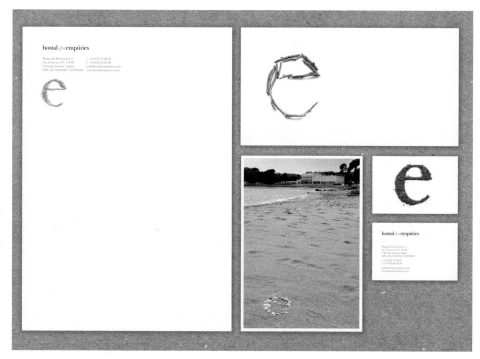

HOSTAL EMPÚRIES

by: espluga+associates

for: Hostal Empúries

in: L'Escala, Girona, Spain

Espluga+associates created the visual identity for **HOSTAL EMPÚRIES**, the first LEED (Leadership in Energy and Environmental Design) certified hotel in Europe. In keeping with the hotel's commitment to environmentally sustainable materials and practices, the identity design uses elements from the hotel's natural environment for the "e" used on printed materials.

ORGANOID TECHNOLOGIES

DIE ORGANOIDE® PLATTFORM TECHNOLOGIE
ERMÖGLICHT DIE KOSTENGÜNSTIGE HERSTELLUNG
VON FREIFORMOBJEKTEN AUF BASIS EINER VIELZAHL
VON NACHWACHSENDEN ROHSTOFFEN.

NOFRONTIERE◉ CAST

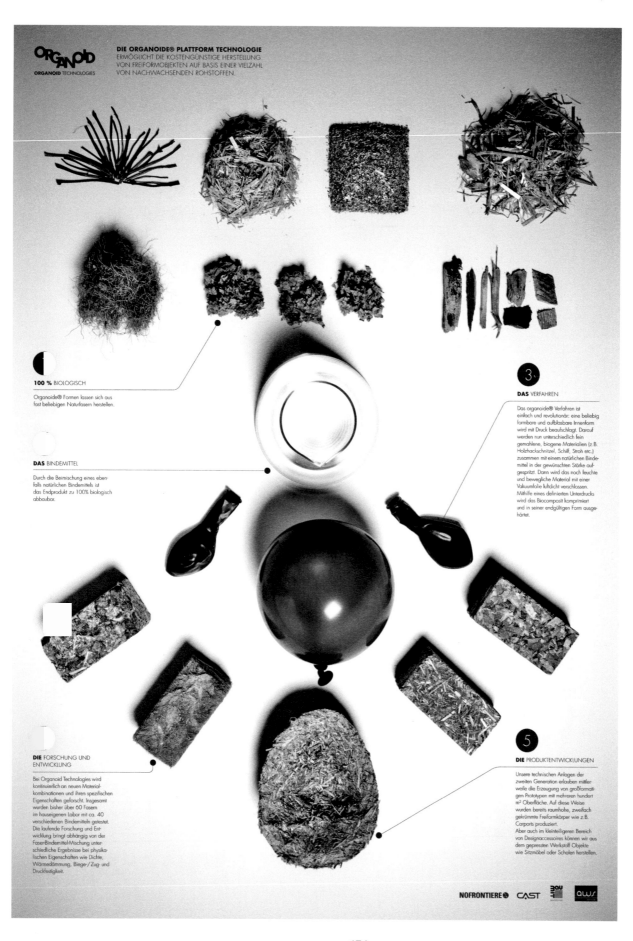

ORGANOID
ORGANOID TECHNOLOGIES

DIE ORGANOIDE® PLATTFORM TECHNOLOGIE
ERMÖGLICHT DIE KOSTENGÜNSTIGE HERSTELLUNG
VON FREIFORMOBJEKTEN AUF BASIS EINER VIELZAHL
VON NACHWACHSENDEN ROHSTOFFEN.

100 % BIOLOGISCH

Organoide® Formen lassen sich aus
fast beliebigen Naturfasern herstellen.

DAS BINDEMITTEL

Durch die Beimischung eines ebenfalls natürlichen Bindemittels ist
das Endprodukt zu 100% biologisch
abbaubar.

DIE FORSCHUNG UND
ENTWICKLUNG

Bei Organoid Technologies wird
kontinuierlich an neuen Material-
kombinationen und ihren spezifischen
Eigenschaften geforscht. Insgesamt
wurden bisher über 60 Fasern
im hauseigenen Labor mit ca. 40
verschiedenen Bindemitteln getestet.
Die laufende Forschung und Entwicklung bringt abhängig von der
Faser-Bindemittel-Mischung unter-
schiedliche Ergebnisse bei physika-
lischen Eigenschaften wie Dichte,
Wärmedämmung, Biege-/Zug- und
Druckfestigkeit.

③ **DAS** VERFAHREN

Das organoide® Verfahren ist
einfach und revolutionär: eine beliebig
formbare und aufblasbare Innenform
wird mit Druck beaufschlagt. Darauf
werden nun unterschiedlich fein
gemahlene, biogene Materialien (z.B.
Holzhackschnitzel, Schilf, Stroh etc.)
zusammen mit einem natürlichen Bindemittel in der gewünschten Stärke auf-
gespritzt. Dann wird das noch feuchte
und bewegliche Material mit einer
Vakuumfolie luftdicht verschlossen.
Mithilfe eines definierten Unterdrucks
wird das Biocomposit komprimiert
und in seiner endgültigen Form ausge-
härtet.

⑤ **DIE** PRODUKTENTWICKLUNGEN

Unsere technischen Anlagen der
zweiten Generation erlauben mittler-
weile die Erzeugung von großformati-
gen Prototypen mit mehreren hundert
m² Oberfläche. Auf diese Weise
wurden bereits raumhohe, zweifach
gekrümmte Freiformkörper wie z.B.
Carports produziert.
Aber auch im kleinteiligeren Bereich
von Designaccessoires können wir aus
dem gepressten Werkstoff Objekte
wie Sitzmöbel oder Schalen herstellen.

NOFRONTIERE CAST bau aws

154

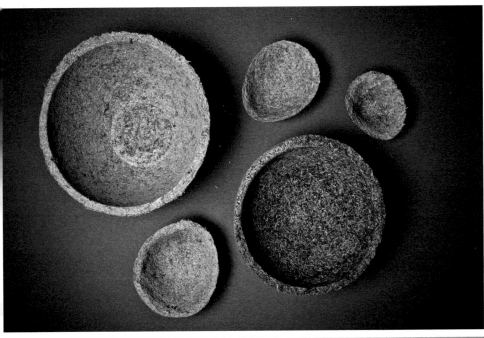

ORGANOID TECHNOLOGIES

ORGANOID

by: Nofrontiere Design //
Martha Luczak, Isolde
Fitzel

for: Organoid Technologies

in: Wenns, Austria

The fundamental idea behind the **ORGANOID** technology is based on the beneficial effect that flowing, organic free-form building components produce on the observer. Believing that the well-being and life quality of an individual in his or her working or living environment can be significantly improved with primal, organic forms and the employment of natural materials, Martin Jehart and Christoph Egger founded Organoid Technologies to develop ecologically friendly, sustainable, and affordable solutions with renewable raw materials as the basis. Commissioned to develop corporate and product design solutions for the young, forward-looking company, Nofrontiere focused on materiality: The patented **ORGANOID** manufacturing process enables the fabrication of eco-friendly products from natural fibres. Presented like raw laboratory probes to communicate the forward-looking research and development approach, those finely grounded biogenic materials become key elements of Nofrontier's unpretentious design. Presented on a clinical white backdrop are small batches of grasses, biological fibres, and agricultural waste; the straightforward graphic language allows for their natural appeal to speak for itself. In the actual manufacturing process, the materials are being sprayed on individually designed negative forms together with a natural binder; a specific vacuum is then crucial for the hardening of the positive form. The ongoing research and development ensures important physical properties such as density, insulation, bending strength, tensile strength, and compressive strength, making the material a serious alternative to synthetics for designer and architects.

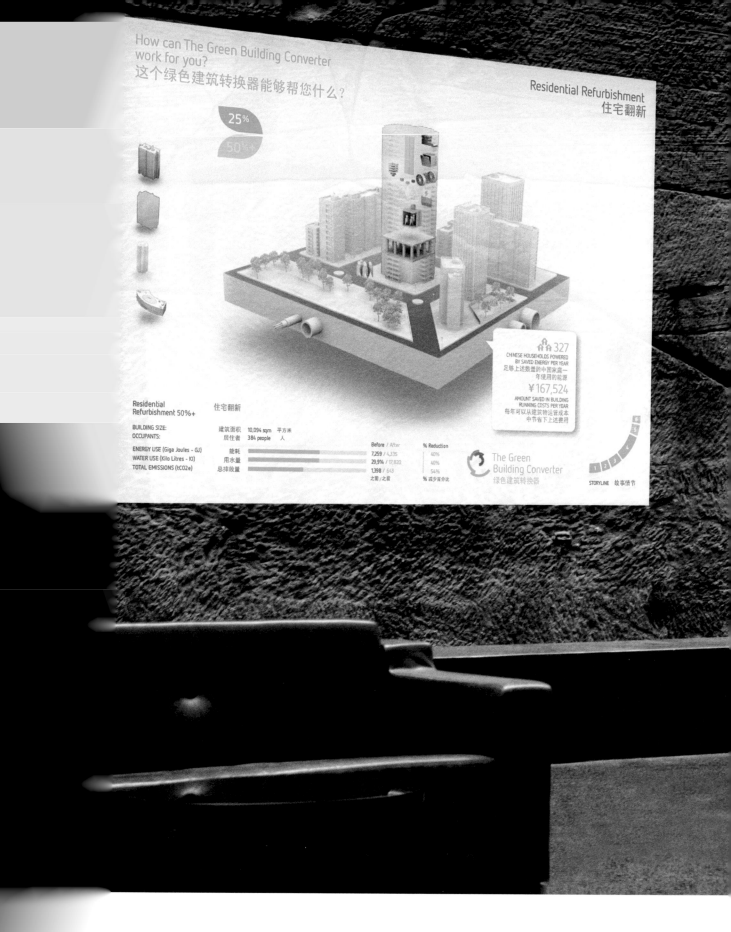

LEND LEASE SUSTAINABILITY SUITE

by: Collider //
Andrew van der Westhuyzen
for: Lend Lease
in: Australia

Collider has produced a range of communication systems for the global developer Lend Lease. Their interactive Green Building Converter guided users through the process of green development and demonstrated how Lend Lease could help developers and owners reduce the CO_2 emissions of their buildings. The **LEND LEASE SUSTAINABILITY SUITE** included a new visual system, pictograms, iconography, and the online Sustainability Explorer, which uses existing office, residential, and retail buildings to demonstrate the health and economic benefits of green buildings using greenhouse gas emissions, energy consumption, and water demand.

The Toolkit Categories
Colour

There are 14 unique Toolkit Categories designed to cover every facet of the sustainability business.

 Energy Sources

 Energy Efficiency

 Water

 Building Materials

 Waste

 Health & Wellbeing

 Nature

 Social

 Economy

 Transport

 Communities

 Shared Infrastructure

 Triple Bottom Line

 No CO$_2$

Colour Use

 R-255 M-10 G-221 Y-100 B-0

R-202 C-25 G-219 Y-100 B-42

R-22 C-70 G-185 M-5 B-237

R-175 C-30 G-222 Y-15 B-220

 R-124 C-40 G-189 K-15 B-217

R-175 C-30 G-222 K-15 B-220

R-77 C-71 G-133 M-42 B-197

R-226 C-7 G-57 M-93 B-39 Y-100

R-51 C-85 G-125 M-42 B-95 Y-78

 R-77 C-71 G-133 M-42 B-197

R-243 M-10 G-112 Y-100 B-33

R-20 C-72 G-187 Y-38 B-176

R-113 C-40 G-229 Y-7 B-243

R-17 C-65 G-187 M-2 B-204 K-18

 R-124 C-40 G-189 K-15 B-217

R-77 C-71 G-133 M-42 B-197

R-226 C-7 G-57 M-93 B-39 Y-100

R-51 C-85 G-125 M-42 B-95 Y-78

 R-202 C-25 G-219 Y-100 B-42

R-77 C-71 G-133 M-42 B-197

R-243 M-70 G-112 Y-100 B-33

 R-202 C-25 G-219 Y-100 B-42

R-217 K-15 G-217 B-217

R-110 K-60 G-110 B-110

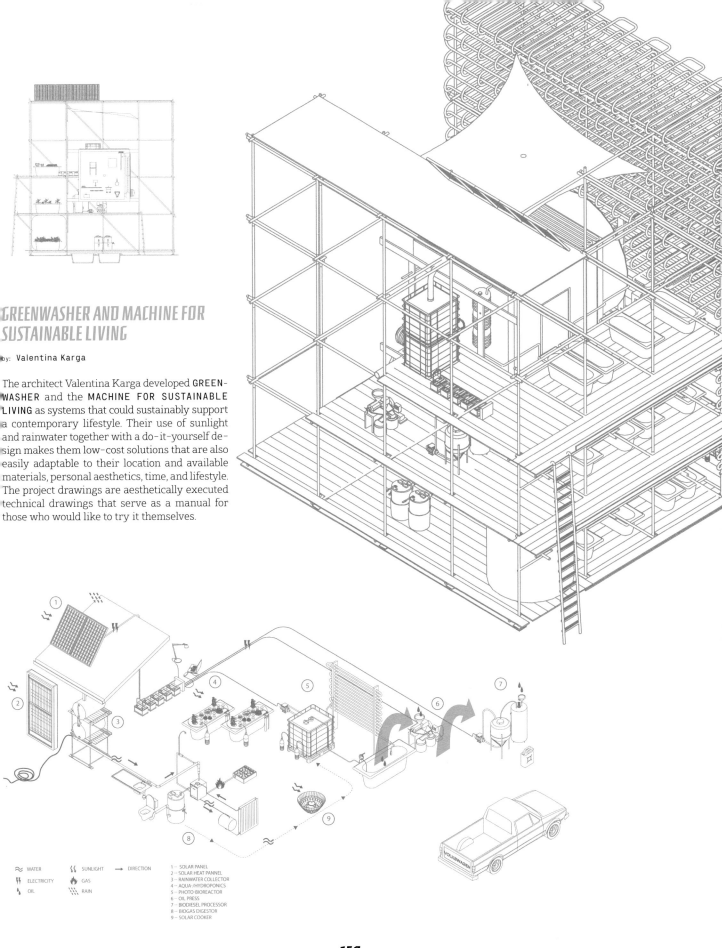

GREENWASHER AND MACHINE FOR SUSTAINABLE LIVING

by: Valentina Karga

The architect Valentina Karga developed GREEN-WASHER and the MACHINE FOR SUSTAINABLE LIVING as systems that could sustainably support a contemporary lifestyle. Their use of sunlight and rainwater together with a do-it-yourself design makes them low-cost solutions that are also easily adaptable to their location and available materials, personal aesthetics, time, and lifestyle. The project drawings are aesthetically executed technical drawings that serve as a manual for those who would like to try it themselves.

≈ WATER   ⸨⸨ SUNLIGHT   → DIRECTION

⫙ ELECTRICITY   ⸙ GAS

⸫ OIL   ⸬ RAIN

1 – SOLAR PANEL
2 – SOLAR HEAT PANNEL
3 – RAINWATER COLLECTOR
4 – AQUA-/HYDROPONICS
5 – PHOTO-BIOREACTOR
6 – OIL PRESS
7 – BIODIESEL PROCESSOR
8 – BIOGAS DIGESTOR
9 – SOLAR COOKER

SEČOVLJE SALINA NATURE PARK

by: Lukatarina
for: SOLINE Pridelava soli
in: Slovenia

The SOLINE Pridelava soli produces fine salt and other high-quality products in the traditional manner. Dedicated to protecting and preserving the natural and cultural heritage within **SEČOVLJE SALINA NATURE PARK**, the company approached the sustainably-minded designers Lukatarina to develop a graphic solution that would promote the park, which is not only a place of salt production but also home to a number of birds, other animals, and salt loving-plants. The resulting identity is based on a set of illustrations that merge the park's facets as a place of salt production and integral nature reserve. Inspired by the friendly retro feel of the existing logo, a range of figurative elements can be used independently or as an integrated pattern.

CLIMATE CAMP POSTER ^{opposite page}

by: Amelia Gregory, Mia Overgaard
for: Climate Camp
in: London, U.K.

Designed for the 2009 Climate Camp, a one-week series of climate and sustainable living educational workshops that took place on Blackheath in London, the colorful poster draws attention to the event's agenda. Key ideas like sustainable living, community spirit, anti-capitalist mindset, and direct action for change are translated into a set of vivid pictograms. Conceived by a designer who was found via an open brief and who then worked with Amelia Gregory to finalize the concept, the image was selected by a design working group within Climate Camp, to be used on walls, flags, stickers, and bunting across London.

160

10:10 GLOBAL

by: 10:10global.org

in: U.K.

10:10 is based on one simple idea: uniting the world to cut its carbon emissions by 10 percent per year—starting now. Its participants—individuals, businesses, schools, and sports clubs from 171 countries—sign up and receive tips and tools for cutting carbon emissions. 10:10 also sponsors related projects: a social Web app to help users reduce their carbon footprint; Lighter Later, an initiative to set clocks for more sunlight during waking hours; and Solar Schools, which helps schools raise money for clean energy systems.

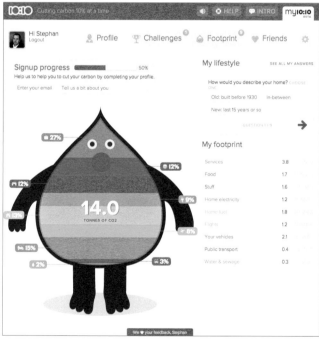

PLANET-UPCYCLING LOGO

by: RADEKAL KNZPT & DSGN //
    Radek Goldstein-Kubicki
for: Plup — Planet-Upcycling
in: Düsseldorf, Germany

Planet-Upcycling, a start-up business focusing on sales and distribution of upcycling products, approached RADEKAL KNZPT & DSGN to develop a contemporary and memorable corporate identity. Reducing the somewhat unwieldy company name to a catchy "Plup," the designers created a set of idiosyncratic logos: pieced together from various objects and elements, the series of pictogram-like illustrations reflects the concept of upcycling in a playful manner.

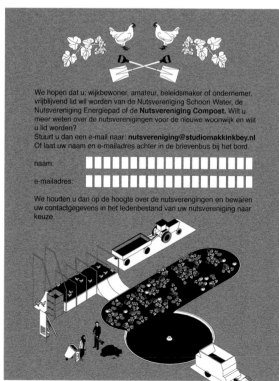

We hopen dat u; wijkbewoner, amateur, beleidsmaker of ondernemer, vrijblijvend lid wil worden van de Nutsvereniging Schoon Water, de Nutsvereniging Energiepad of de **Nutsvereniging Compost.** Wilt u meer weten over de nutsverenigingen voor de nieuwe woonwijk en wilt u lid worden?
Stuurt u dan een e-mail naar: **nutsvereniging@studiomakkinkbey.nl**
Of laat uw naam en e-mailadres achter in de brievenbus bij het bord.

naam:

e-mailadres:

We houden u dan op de hoogte over de nutsverengingen en bewaren uw contactgegevens in het ledenbestand van uw nutsvereniging naar keuze.

FOODPRINT ERASMUSVELD

by: Studio Makkink & Bey
for: Stroom Den Haag
in: Netherlands

Erasmusveld is an urban development area in The Hague that is set out to become a highly sustainable and self-sufficient neighborhood. The idea, as envisioned by Stroom and Studio Makkink & Bey, was to reverse the conventional process of architectural development so that it is not defined by technical layouts but by its social infrastructure. Teaming up with Makkink & Bey to develop a design strategy that would perform as an incentive for sustainability, they continued to work on their vision of a Society of Engagement: Based on a previous concept, the idea took the shape of Utility Associations, set up to establish solid bonds to support the sharing of responsibilities and caring for shared space. Focusing on the issue of food, food production, and waste management, the Utility Associations were structured around three themes: compost, water, and energy. Based on the belief that only an engaged, collectively organized society can frame future cities with enough viability and resilience to react to radical changes, Erasmusveld represents the state of the art of sustainable living. Self-organization, alliances between public and private parties, collective responsibility, collective effort, and collective results are the engines to keep the vision alive.

ALLOTINABOX BRAND PACKAGING: BOX AND CONTENTS

by: ilovedust
for: ALLOTINABOX
in: U.K.

On the mission to encourage anyone to get growing, even in the smallest urban flats in the heart of the city, ALLOTINABOX produces and delivers practical, space saving grow-your-own kits. Allotted in the box are not only seeds, but also a set of useful tools and gardening equipment to get everyone from the seasoned grower to the young professional with little or no green experience going. With their brand, website, and full range of products and packaging designed by ilovedust, ALLOTINABOX promotes sustainable living and the idea of harvesting fresh fruit, vegetables, and herbs at home as a fashionable, fun thing to do.

BOATANIC

by: **Damian O'Sullivan Design //**
Damian O'Sullivan

in: **Netherlands**

The **BOATANIC** is a solution for reducing the environmental impact of transporting food over long distances. It converts discarded Dutch tourist boats into floating gardens that produce herbs, fruit, and vegetables on urban canals and waterways. This produce can then be purchased directly, as a subscription, or delivered by bike to restaurants, while an educational program teaches children about growing their own food. For the convenience of its customers, **BOATANIC**'s daily location and produce selection will be made available on its website and smartphone app. White and green branding makes the boat, its bikes, and its products easy to spot. Simple black and white icons create an equation that explains the key elements of their unusual business plan in a lighthearted way.

JBG BRAND OVERLOOK

by: L A N D //
Ryan Rhodes
for: Johnson's Backyard Garden
in: Austin, USA

Johnson's Backyard Garden began in 2004 as a backyard garden in a residential neighborhood, where the owners grew produce for sale at their local Austin, Texas, farmers' market. By 2010, they had expanded to larger plots of land and found themselves operating a 1,000-member community supported agriculture program, or CSA. Wanting to solidify their brand and reach more people in the community, they hired the Austin design studio L A N D to create an identity that reflects the farm's local, do-it-yourself roots. The graphics, created from organic materials, have a hand-stamped quality to them. L A N D also designed a special shareholder certificate for the CSA members. The spirit of the marketing materials reflects the farm's commitment to operating locally with organic products.

WONDERWATER CAFÉ

by: Jane Withers, Kari Korkman, Aalto University,
Iina-Karoliina Välilä, Tiina Koivusalo
in: Beijing, China

WONDERWATER CAFÉ is a pop-up event that explores the relationship between food and water consumption by showing diners the water footprint of their food. A menu designed as an infographic presents the cafe's food options. Each item is represented by an icon that varies in size depending on its water footprint. The food is then broken down into more detailed information about its water production needs. By presenting diners with information in this way, they can see the hidden water usage in their food and make responsible choices in the future.

STOP THE WATER WHILE USING ME!

by: T.D.G. Vertriebs
for: STOP THE WATER WHILE USING ME!
in: Hamburg, Germany

STOP THE WATER WHILE USING ME! is the first cosmetics range with a clear environmental call to save water. The bio-compatible shampoos, shower gels, soaps, and body lotions are characterized by the simple, handwritten design of their packaging, which makes it immediately clear how easy it is to be environmentally friendly.

家常豆腐
Domestic life bean curd

1,641
升水用于种植大豆以生产豆腐、豆瓣酱和酱油
litres for growing soya beans for bean curd, broad bean sauce and soya sauce

1,061
升水用于养殖肉牛以生产牛肉汤
litres for raising cattle used to make beef soup

300
升水用于种植蘑菇
litres for growing mushrooms

148
升水用于种植豆瓣酱的另一种原材料：水稻
litres for growing rice for broad bean sauce

270
升水用于生产炸豆腐、制作酱油所需的葵花籽油
litres for sunflower oil for soya sauce and to fry the tofu

74
升水用于生产料酒、盐、醋、洋葱、生姜、大蒜、五香粉和淀粉
litres for cooking wine, salt, vinegar, spring onion, ginger, garlic, various spices and starch

3,494
升水用于制作这道菜肴
litres of water for this dish

▲ =150 L

水煮肉片
Poached pork slices in chili water

3,291
升水用于养猪
litres for raising pigs

710
升水用于种植大豆及发酵蚕豆
litres for growing soya beans and fermented broad beans

600
升水用于生产肉汤
litres for meat soup

148
升水用于种植水稻
litres for rice

120
升水用于种植向日葵以生产葵花籽油
litres for growing sunflowers for sunflower oil

96
升水用于生产盐、五香粉、料酒、淀粉、花椒、辣椒、大蒜、姜和鸡精
litres for salt, various spices, cooking wine, starch, chillies, Szechuan pepper, garlic, ginger and chicken essence

67
升水用于生产白糖
litres for sugar

57
升水用于种植大白菜和大蒜
litres for Chinese cabbage and Welsh onion

The water footprint of pork is roughly a third of beef.
猪肉的水足迹差不多是牛肉的三分之一。

5,089
升水用于制作这道菜肴
litres of water for this dish

▲ =150 L

你每天"吃"掉多少水？
how much water do you eat?

天海幻水
wonderwater Tian Hai

WATER RETENTION SQUARE

by: Studio Marco Vermeulen //
    Marco Vermeulen
for: Community of Rotterdam
in: Rotterdam, Netherlands

The city of Rotterdam drains its storm water into an extensive sewer system that is already over capacity. Instead of enlarging the system, Marco Vermeulen proposed a complementary system of water retention squares that function as public spaces when dry and transform into water basins after a heavy downpour. They would filter rainwater into the ground, eventually releasing it through the city's sewage system. His prototype demonstrates squares that double as urban sports facilities; the square is separated into different basins/sport fields that would flood successively, depending on the amount of rain. This versatile solution means that even during the rainy season, most of the sport fields could still be used.

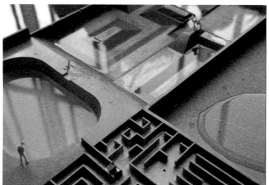

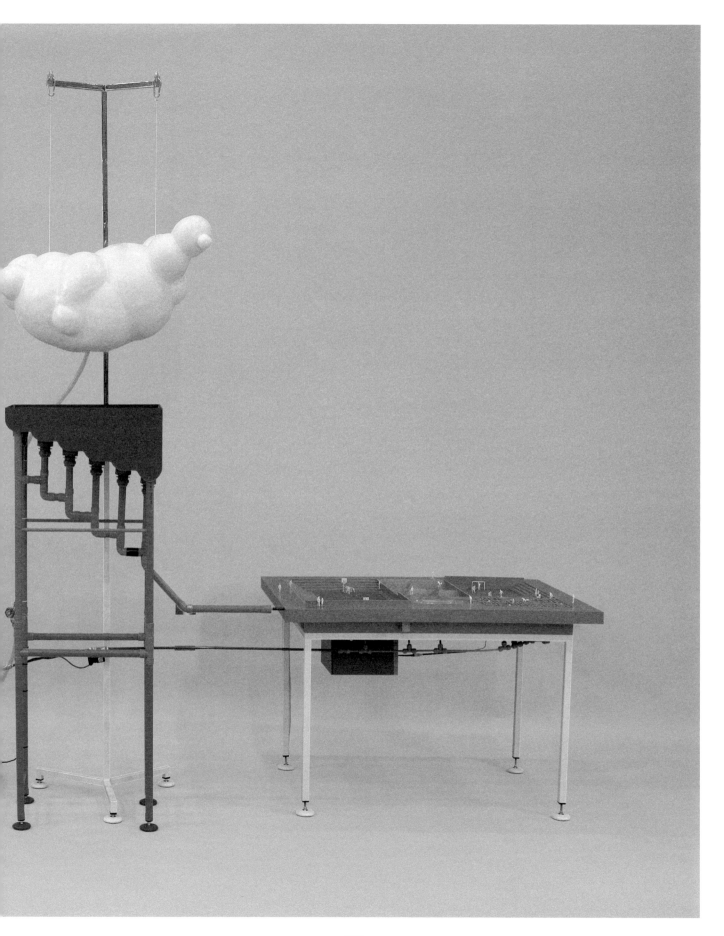

THE TOASTER PROJECT

by: **Thomas Thwaites**
in: **U.K.**

When Thomas Thwaites decided to build a toaster from scratch, his research showed that he would need raw materials such as copper, iron, and nickel. These materials would not only need to be dug out of the ground, but processed, too—a difficult but not impossible task for an individual. The toaster took him nine months to make and cost 250 times more than an average toaster available in the store. Documented with video and later made into a book, the project became a commentary on the consumer's dependence on global industry, and the environmental costs of impossibly cheap and disposable products.

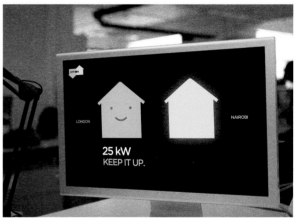

LED ENERGY CONSUMPTION DISPLAY

by: Wieden + Kennedy //
Ray Shaughnessy,
Sophie Bodoh,
Dan Norris, Sophie
Dollar
for: OFF-ON
in: London, U.K.

Wieden + Kennedy's OFF-ON initiative encourages employees to turn off power-hungry appliances as a way of reducing their energy consumption. As an incentive, the savings are tracked and then invested in solar-power panels for a children's home in Nairobi. To keep employees engaged, the agency developed a system with Pell Frishmann engineers that uses real-time energy monitors to show how much energy is in use; what is turned off in London relates directly to what is turned on in Africa. Stickers and signs sit by light switches and appliances as a reminder of the company's symbiotic relationship with the children's home.

ENERGY AWARE CLOCK

by: Interactive Institute

in: Sweden

The **ENERGY AWARE CLOCK** is an electricity meter designed to make energy awareness a part of everyday life. The clock visualizes the daily energy rhythms of the household; when an appliance is switched on, graphs made from the previous day's energy use fade into the background while the current consumption is drawn on top. This makes it possible to compare energy throughout the home over a period of time. With it, each household can measure their energy use—and strive to be more energy efficient.

PHILIPS DESIGN

PHILIPS DESIGN believes that technology and innovation can be used to create sustainable products that enrich lives. That means creating new products for consumers, working on ideas for the future that inspire others to do the same, and contributing to philanthropic projects. Their work encompasses a wide range of sustainable health and environmental products for home, work, personal health, fashion, time management, and travel, making them a leader in sustainability.

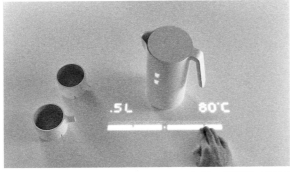

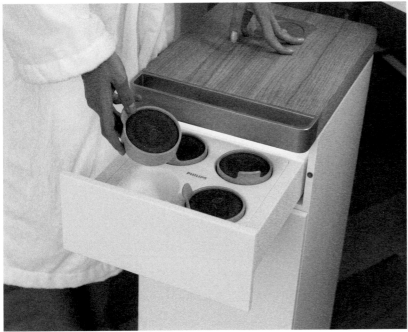

GREEN CUISINE

by: **Philips Design**
in: **Netherlands**

The **GREEN CUISINE** design concept gives consumers a greener cooking experience. This eco-friendly domestic kitchen lets consumers cook, entertain, and enjoy food while reducing energy consumption and optimizing waste management. Sensors sense water amounts and set cooking temperatures accordingly, while its built-in composting system easily disposes of and reuses organics. **GREEN CUISINE** simplifies energy efficiency and gives an insight into future product development for a more sustainable world.

MICROBIAL HOME

by: **Philips Design**

in: **Netherlands**

The **MICROBIAL HOME** probe project is a domestic eco-system that proposes new design solutions for energy, cleaning, food preservation, lighting, and human waste. It uses biological processes to filter, process, and recycle what we conventionally think of as waste: sewage, effluent, garbage, and gray water. It is a set of units that function as a food preparation station—which is also the home's energy source—a larder for fresh food, a beehive, bio-light, apothecary, toilet, and plastic waste upcycler. As a design concept, the **MICROBIAL HOME** is not intended to be a prototype. Instead it facilitates discussion about sustainability solutions.

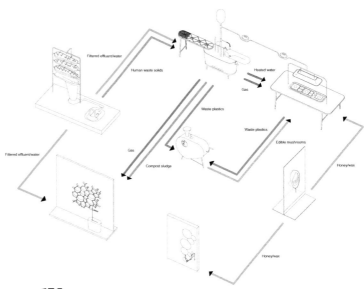

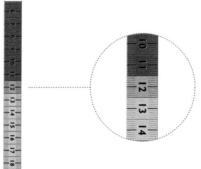

TRUNKY & MONKEY

by: Philips Design
in: Eindhoven, Netherlands

As part of its Fight Malnutrition initiative, Philips created **TRUNKY & MONKEY**, a low-cost and low-tech measuring solution. Specifically developed for under five year-olds, the user-friendly, playful design encourages parents to quickly check their children at home, and children to co-operate in having their measurements taken. Templates can be downloaded from the Internet, printed, and cut out. The strap is then wrapped around the child's mid-upper arm, allowing for parents and non-professional healthcare workers to detect and measure potential malnutrition with ease.

LOW SMOKE CHULHA

by: **Philips Design**

in: **Netherlands, India**

Target users and NGOs developed the **LOW SMOKE CHULHA** cooking stove, which uses biomass fuel to reduce disease caused by smoke inhalation during indoor cooking. Initially introduced in India, it is now also available in African markets. Instead of producing and selling the **CHULHA**, Philips keeps its production sustainable and local through free distribution of the design specifications on lowsmokechulha.com, which also encourages networking and information sharing. The **CHULHA** has received numerous awards including the Bronze IDEA Ecodesign Award 2008, Red Dot Award for Design Concept 2008, and INDEX Award 2009.

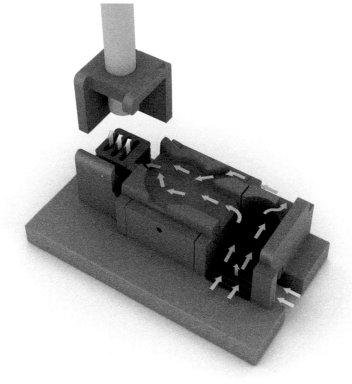

Kleinbauern-Kooperativen in aller Welt betreiben nachhaltige Landwirtschaft.

Der Verein unterstützt soziale und ökonomische Projekte in den Anbaugebieten.

Jede Flasche LemonAid und ChariTea beinhaltet nur biologische und faire Zutaten.

Pro verkaufter Flasche fließt zudem ein fester Betrag an den LemonAid & ChariTea e.V.

LEMONAID & CHARITEA ANNUAL REPORT

by: Jung von Matt //
    Katja Kirchner, Annika Frey,
    Christina Drescher
for: LemonAid & ChariTea
in: Germany

LemonAid uses only organic, fair-trade ingredients in its products and donates a large portion of its sales to aid projects in the countries that supply the ingredients. Rejecting traditional business models that focus solely on profit, they set out to create a business that makes the world a fairer place and produces a high-quality product. Their 2010 annual report reflected these values, using bar graphs in equal portions and presenting employee names in a circle instead of a hierarchy according to position.

LEMONAID+

ChariTea®

MULA TEXTILE SHOPPING BAGS

by: Lukatarina

for: Eco Vitae

in: Ljubljana, Slovenia

An ongoing nonprofit collaboration between Lukatarina and Eco Vitae, the Mula brand and initiative aims to raise awareness about the problem of plastic bags. With the MULA TEXTILE SHOPPING BAG Collection they offer a practical and stylish alternative. A bit of background info on the bags' paper straps encourages customers to refuse plastic bags when shopping. Pointing to the fact that the issue is for everyone, Lukatarina developed a variety of designs to speak to different target groups. The latest collection, MulaMundus, is composed of three silk-screen pattern designs.

Življenjski cikel vrečke iz blaga

mula.

SUROVINA
RASTLINSKA VLAKNA RAZLIČNIH VRST
... so obnovljivi in naravni vir surovin za izdelavo blaga. Za vzgojo nekaterih vrst je potrebno namakanje, gnojenje in škropljenje. Danes se mnogi pridelovalci odločajo za organsko pridelavo rastlin, brez uporabe okolju in rastlinam nevarnih kemikalij.

transport

PROIZVODNJA
TISOČLETJA STAR POSTOPEK ...
... omogoča izdelavo tekstilnega blaga iz rastlinskih vlaken. Glavni koraki so predenje, tkanje, krojenje in šivanje. Občasno je v procesu potrebno dodati mehčala in druga aditive za izboljšanje kakovosti blaga.

transport

UPORABA
ENA VREČKA – VEČ LET
Vrečke iz blaga so zasnovane trajnostno. Isto vrečko lahko uporabljate več let. Edini pogoj je, da jo vzamete s seboj v trgovino. Vrečke so pralne, zanje pa je značilna dolga doba uporabnosti in kratka doba razgradnje.

transport

RAZGRADNJA
BIORAZGRADLJIVO IN RECIKLABILNO
Vrečke iz blaga v naravnem okolju je popolnoma biorazgradljiva. Blago je organska snov, primerna za prehrano mikroorganizmov v tleh. Le-ti vrečko razgradijo do osnovnih elementov, ki lahko ponovno vstopijo v življenjski cikel rastlin. V tem primeru odpadkov ni.

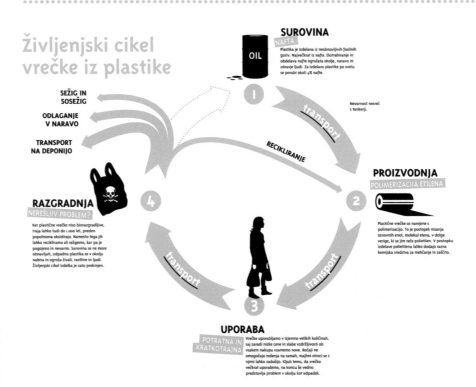

Življenjski cikel vrečke iz plastike

SUROVINA
NAFTA
Plastika je izdelana iz neobnovljivih fosilnih goriv. Največkrat iz nafte. Ekstrahiranje in obdelava nafte ogrožata okolje, naravo in zdravje ljudi. Za izdelavo plastike po svetu se porabi okoli 4% nafte.

OIL

transport

Nevarnost nesreč s tankerji.

RECIKLIRANJE

PROIZVODNJA
POLIMERIZACIJA ETILENA
Plastične vrečke so narejene s polimerizacijo. To je postopek nizanja osnovnih enot, molekul etena, v dolge verige, ki se jim reče polietilen. V postopku izdelave polietilena lahko dodajo razna kemijska sredstva za mehčanje in zaščito.

transport

UPORABA
POTRATNA IN KRATKOTRAJNA
Vrečke uporabljamo v izjemno velikih količinah, saj zaradi nizke cene in slabe vzdržljivosti ob vsakem nakupu vzamemo nove. Ročaji ne omogočajo nošenja na ramah, majhni otroci se z njimi lahko zadušijo. Kljub temu, da vrečko večkrat uporabimo, na koncu še vedno predstavlja problem v okolju kot odpadek.

transport

RAZGRADNJA
NEREŠLJIV PROBLEM?
Ker plastične vrečke niso biorazgradljive, traja lahko tudi do 1.000 let, preden popolnoma oksidirajo. Namesto tega jih lahko recikliramo ali sežgemo, kar pa je pogojno in nevarno. Surovine se ne more obnavljati, odpadna plastika se v okolju nabira in ogroža živali, rastline in ljudi. Življenjski cikel izdelka je zato prekinjen.

SEŽIG IN SOSEŽIG

ODLAGANJE V NARAVO

TRANSPORT NA DEPONIJO

LET EFFICIENCY REIGN.*

* IF EVERY U.S. HOUSEHOLD INSTALLED WATER-EFFICIENT AIR-CONDITIONERS, FRIDGES AND OTHER APPLIANCES, WE WOULD SAVE MORE THAN 11.3 TRILLION LITERS OF WATER A YEAR.

TAKE A STEP IN THE RIGHT DIRECTION. VISIT LEVI.COM
TO SEE HOW WE'RE FINDING WAYS TO CARE FOR OUR PLANET.

SAVE WATER:
SHOWER WITH A FRIEND.*

*A FIVE-MINUTE SHOWER CAN USE UP TO 95 LITERS OF WATER.

TAKE A STEP IN THE RIGHT DIRECTION. VISIT LEVI.COM
TO SEE HOW WE'RE FINDING WAYS TO CARE FOR OUR PLANET.

LEVI'S WATER > LESS

by: MYOO Agency, Johnny Lighthands
for: Levi Strauss USA
in: U.K., USA

Denim has a larger negative effect on the environment than one might expect. The growing and processing of cotton using pesticides, herbicides, and gallons of water; the application of dyes that are potentially hazardous; and the liquids and chemicals that are needed to color the denim blue or black and to make the jeans look worn— all this adds up to a huge footprint. Expressing a sense of responsibility Levi's decided to tackle the sustainability challenge. Setting great store by economic water consumption, they support the Better Cotton Initiative to encourage thousands of cotton farmers in dozens of countries where cotton is grown to use less water. They develop their own water-saving strategy to be applied in the finishing process of LEVI'S WATER > LESS, a sustainable range of jeans designed to help reduce global water wastage. And they team up with MYOO and British illustrator Johnny Lighthands to bring the message to life: an educational campaign of over 30 illustrated posters and two comic strips, starring a range of water-conserving creatures in Lighthands's unique free-hand style. On protest with placards claiming to share showers and reuse old water for their houseplants, the slightly naïve, but certainly lovable brand ambassadors turn the serious issue into entertaining sequences.

LEAKS ARE WEAK.*

* FIXING A LEAK WILL SAVE YOU 2,120 LITERS A MONTH.

TAKE A STEP IN THE RIGHT DIRECTION. VISIT LEVI.COM
TO SEE HOW WE'RE FINDING WAYS TO CARE FOR OUR PLANET.

DONT WASH THE STORIES OUT OF YOUR LEVI'S® JEANS.

TAKE A STEP IN THE RIGHT DIRECTION. VISIT LEVI.COM
TO SEE HOW WE'RE FINDING WAYS TO CARE FOR OUR PLANET.

LEMON TRI IDENTITY AND ANIMATED PRESENTATION

by: Atelier Antoine Corbineau //
    Antoine Corbineau
for: Lemon tri
in: France

The French company Lemon tri is deeply committed to environmental issues. They specialize in sorting recyclable waste in schools, universities, and corporations and provide an incentive program for users that rewards them with gifts or the opportunity to make charitable donations. Lemon tri also compensates for the CO_2 emissions from its vehicles through a partnership with Tree-Nation. Antoine Corbineau's hand-drawn illustrations are an integral part of Lemon tri's identity. They serve as vivacious pictorial explanations of what Lemon tri does and what it believes in.

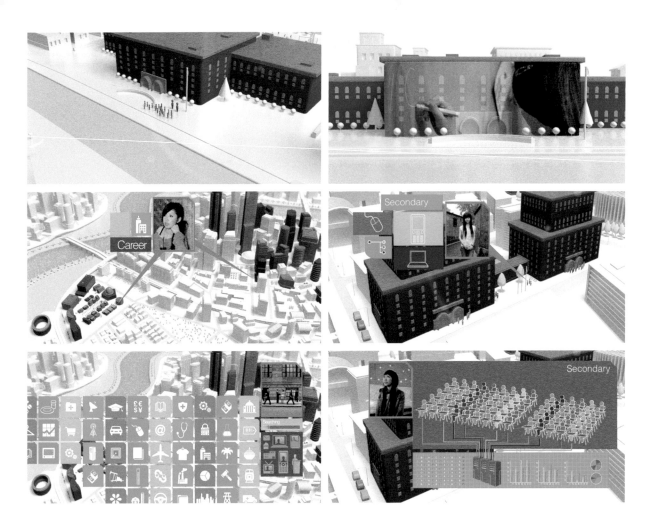

IBM SMARTER PLANET CAMPAIGN — "LET'S BUILD A SMARTER PLANET"

by: Ogilvy & Mather New York
for: IBM
in: Worldwide

Developed by Ogilvy & Mather New York, the **SMARTER PLANET CAMPAIGN** seeks to position IBM as the global business and technology leader that works with the world's great governments, companies, thinkers, and doers to change the way the world works. Supporting the launch of their "smart planet" agenda that set the premise and demonstrates real and tangible ways IBM is helping to make the world work better, the company launched a series of print ads to run in the opinion-editorial section of major newspapers. Structured around a variety of specific areas, each ad featured a **SMARTER PLANET** Icon to creatively present IBM's point of view on how the world currently works and how it can work smarter.

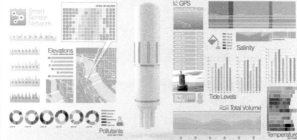

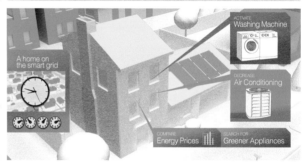

THE SMARTER CITY

by: Ogilvy & Mather New York, Firstborn //
Mike Hahn, Ryan Blank, Susan Westre
for: IBM
in: Worldwide

IBM's **SMARTER CITY** is a virtual, composite place built from the smartest parts and systems of leading cities from around the world. The platform of innovation and new thinking aims to communicate the fact that smart, sustainable solutions are by no means utopian: all featured technology is in action in the world today, innovations born of partnerships with IBM. Built to be understood by a 10-year-old and challenge an expert at the same time, the virtual journey navigates through 11 richly animated chapters, introducing the audience to a city that, like so many around the world, strives to overcome the challenges of urban life. Exploring significant issues across education, transportation, economic welfare, security, healthcare, and the environment, the animation unveils quite a few smart answers that are based on case studies, solutions, and services from IBM that are already being applied across the world.

Change by Us NYC is a place to share ideas, create projects, discover resources, and make our city better.

CHANGE BY US NYC

by: Local Projects
for: CEOs for Cities, Local Projects
in: New York, USA

CHANGE BY US helps New Yorkers turn their environmental ideas into action. Using both text messaging and the nyc.changeby.us website, New Yorkers submit their ideas and solutions for a more sustainable city. The website then helps participants form project groups and connect to existing city resources and community organizations. Ideas and suggestions are displayed on post-it notes, which gives the website a friendly, community atmosphere instead of the anonymous feeling of a typical user forum.

THE CIVIL DEBATE WALL

by: Local Projects
for: Bob Graham Center for Public Service
in: Gainesville, USA

THE CIVIL DEBATE WALL is an innovative social media tool for students, teachers, and citizens at the University of Florida's Bob Graham Center for Public Service. Large touch screens, a texting system, and a website create a seamless interactive experience that actively engages users in debates about local, national, and international issues. As users post their opinions, keywords are analyzed to see where the majority agreement lies. The project design requires each user to register and supply a photo with their username, making THE CIVIL DEBATE WALL function more like a social media network, where issues can be debated person-to-person instead of anonymously. Funding for THE CIVIL DEBATE WALL was provided by a grant from the Knight Foundation.

OPEN PLANET IDEAS

by: Sony Europe

n: U.K.

Developed and ran by Sony Europe in partnership with WWF and IDEO, the OPEN PLANET IDEAS initiative encourages the online community to come up with ideas to repurpose existing technology to solve social and environmental challenges. With +U, an accompanying mobile application that makes one-off volunteering quicker, easier, and more social, Sony received hundreds of brilliant ideas from across the world. OPEN PLANET IDEAS is part of Sony's broader focus on the role technology can play in living more sustainable lives. Presented in a bright, straightforward design, the project was fuelled by the inspirational engagement of OPEN PLANET IDEAS community members who collaborated enthusiastically throughout the different phases in the project.

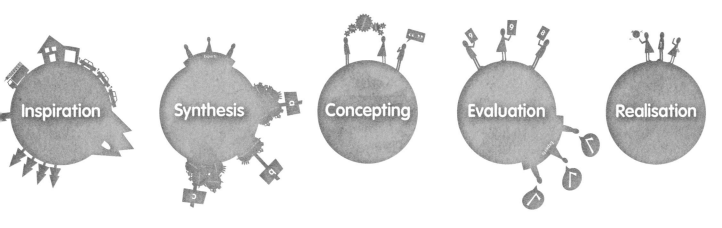

CHAPTER 4

MOVEMENT WITHOUT A NAME

For years, organizations, institutions, and individual initiatives have made it their task to compile an "operating manual for the Earth."[1] U.S. economist Paul Hawken describes it as a movement without a name. Yet the big transformation toward sustainable societies has not yet set in.[2] The hope that a large movement capable of conveying the tasks to broader parts of society would emerge has not been fulfilled until now. Communicating knowledge and facts is already hard enough, but putting theory to practice, applying discourse to everyday life, and turning thought into action form the tasks that distinguish success from failure. Design has the potential of making topics of sustainability experienceable. It can prepare them in such a way that they fascinate people and gain attractiveness. In this manner, design and sustainability communication could provide the leverage to truly and continuously change lifestyles and attitudes.

John Maynard Keynes rightly noted that it is not all too difficult to develop new concepts and strategies; what is much harder is to forget old routines and models.[3] For this reason, one of the most important preconditions for successful sustainability communication will be to make the interrelations between our habits, our daily actions, and their effects on the environment and our fellow humans comprehensible and perceptible by the senses. True change starts with little things, in the family, in one's direct surroundings; with do-it-yourself projects, support-your-local-

community activities or urban gardening. These actions require role models, real persons and projects, tangible and experienceable examples. A will only arises when people are moved by something—in their hearts.[4]

Environmental problems are problems of perception. On the following pages, we therefore present examples of events and exhibitions that have succeeded in sharpening this perception. Projects that use interactive elements to allow complex and often abstract

DESIGN HAS THE POTENTIAL OF MAKING TOPICS OF SUSTAINABILITY EXPERIENCEABLE.

information to be experienced by the senses, that touch and enthuse people. Communities need enthusiasm. It gets things going and brings people to their goal. Enthusiasm is contagious—this is something we are familiar with from concerts or sporting events. The objective is to involve people, to put them in the mood for finding solutions that they deem personally desirable. In the sense of Dominic Veken, the crucial task will be to give rise to a real culture of enthusiasm that plants euphoria in the community's collective memory.[5]

An exhibition shows visions of a future urban life that make it desirable for people. A short event becomes the talk of the town, a small idea becomes an initiative. Visitors and participants turn into multipliers, ambassadors, and carriers of new, viable, and sustainable ideas. With these kinds of images in

one's mind, heart, and soul, even a small group of people can evolve into a large movement, in the sense of what American anthropologist Margaret Mead once said: "Never doubt that a small group of thoughtful, committed citizens can change the world; indeed, it's the only thing that ever has."

The movement without a name has no symbols and no leaders, as we are familiar with from other movements such as the anti-nuclear-power movement or the peace movements. The topic may simply be too complex; the industrial revolution did not have a face or a sign either. Large-scale social transformations must be supported by many. Sustainability communication can contribute to this. We have brought together projects that arouse precisely this enthusiasm because they motivate people to participate, invite them to try things out, and offer them the possibility to gain a constructive experience with the aid of interactive elements. Sustainability communication is convincing due to its complexity, creativity, and diversity. That is what makes it exciting and rousing for all members of society; children and parents, teachers, scientists, entrepreneurs, and politicians are all addressed in the most various ways. Each and everyone of us can therefore become committed and finally take action.

FOOTNOTES

1. See Hawken 1999
2. See Linz 2012
3. See WBGU 2011
4. See Meyer-Abich 1990
5. See Veken 2009

LIST OF LITERATURE

Hawken, Paul (1999): Natural Capitalism, Boston: Little, Brown and Co.

Linz, Manfred (2012): Wie lernen Gesellschaften - heute?, Wuppertal: Wuppertal Institut für Klima, Umwelt, Energie

Meyer-Abich, Klaus Michael (1990): Aufstand für die Natur, München: Carl Hanser Verlag

Veken, Dominic (2009): Ab jetzt Begeisterung, Hamburg: Murmann Verlag

Wissenschaftlicher Beirat der Bundesregierung Globale Umweltveränderungen (WBGU) (2011): Welt im Wandel - Gesellschaftsvertrag für eine große Transformation, Berlin

BUILDING FOR THE 2000-WATT SOCIETY: THE STATE OF AFFAIRS

by: Raffinerie AG für Gestaltung, Holzer Kobler
Architekturen
for: City of Zurich
in: Zurich, Switzerland

The 2000-Watt Society aims to reduce the energy usage of first-world citizens to 2,000 watts per year. For the group's 2009 symposium, THE STATE OF AFFAIRS, the city of Zurich commissioned Raffinerie AG für Gestaltung to create an installation in the Selnau electricity substation. The resulting project—an energy mountain split into six color-themed topics including materials and practices and looking at what 2,000 watts can do—emphasizes sustainable building as a key ecological issue. The nine-meter high installation displays pioneering accomplishments of Swiss architecture on 500 cardboard cubes using a color palette inspired by the color gradation of thermographic images. The exhibition was created in cooperation with Holzer Kobler Architekturen.

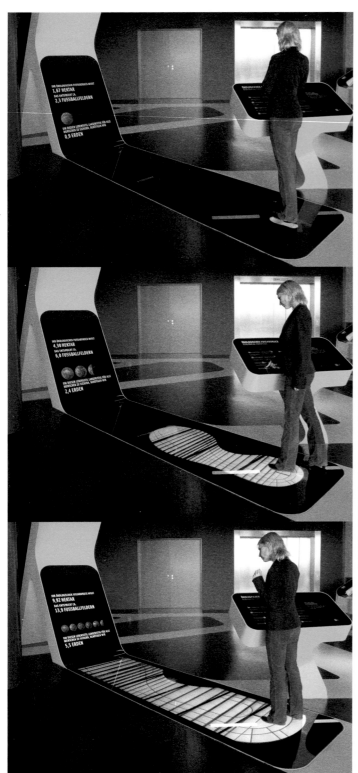

LEVEL GREEN—THE CONCEPT OF SUSTAINABILITY

by: ART+COM

in: Wolfsburg, Germany

The permanent exhibition, **LEVEL GREEN—THE CONCEPT OF SUSTAINABILITY**, at the Autostadt in Wolfsburg bundles information on sustainability in an interactive installation. The exhibition design enlarges computer screens to human proportions, turning the abstract concept of sustainability into a tangible subject. The effects of climate change, the importance of sustainability for industry and society, and future mobility concepts are brought to life using data sculptures, interactive media walls, media installations, and physical artifacts. Personalized media walls let visitors see the environmental impact of their everyday products, while real water demonstrates the international water usage for imports and exports.

POST OIL CITY — DIE STADT NACH DEM ÖL

by: ARCH+, M:AI Museum für Architektur und Ingenieurkunst
NRW, RWTH Aachen, Kolleg Stadt NRW, Ateliers Stark,
kitev — Kultur im Turm e.V. Oberhausen/Berlin
for: M:AI Museum für Architektur und Ingenieurkunst NRW
in: Alsdorf, Germany

Dedicated to pioneering works of architecture and urban
planning, the exhibition **DIE STADT NACH DEM ÖL** (Post
Oil City) renders a rich variety of scenarios that visualize the need for change as an inevitable consequence of
the (expectably very near) end of fossil fuels. Featuring
projects from all over the world, from realized architectural models to seemingly utopian concepts, the curatorial
focus is on sustainability (energy and construction) and
mobility (energy and traffic). Inviting visitors to experience the subject matter first-hand, the exhibition reflects
an atmosphere of departure, which is impressive and
shocking at the same time.

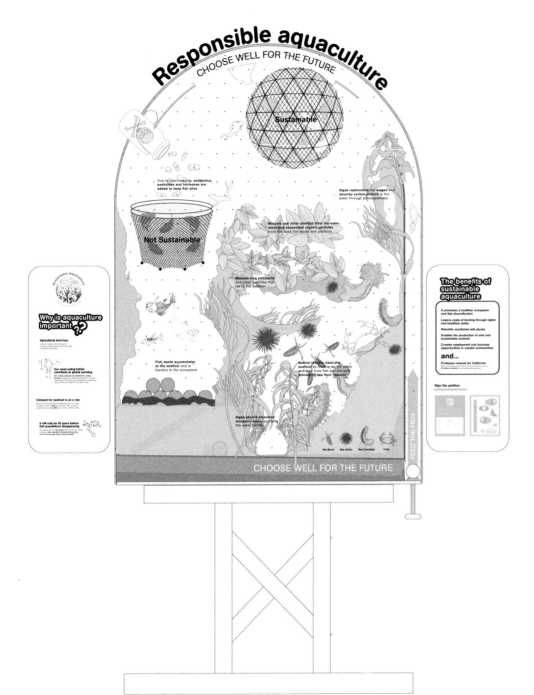

SUSTAINABLE AQUACULTURE — AQUARIUM OF THE PACIFIC: PROJECT COASTAL CRISIS

by: Designmatters at
Art Center College of
Design //
German Aguirre, Derrick
Tan, Jessica Lee
for: Aquarium of the
Pacific, Long Beach, CA
in: Pasadena, USA

The oceans are a precious, shared resource that is critical to our economies and well-being. Dedicated to building and sustaining natural capital—nature—by building and sustaining social capital—the ties between and among people—the Aquarium of the Pacific in Long Beach teamed up with the Designmatters program at Art Center College of Design in Pasadena to set up SUSTAINABLE AQUACULTURE, an accordian pop-up exhibit to spark education and dialogue while visitors eat and relax. Challenged to develop educational campaign strategies to bring public awareness to the impact of sea-level rise in Southern California coastal communities, the students designed an interactive table that communicates facts, figures, and climate change mitigation strategies to inform and alarm people of all ages. An engaging feature for children to learn about sea-level rise is the pinball display: Released balls represent nutrients to be aimed toward the sustainable side of the board; bells and lights go as they tumble through multiple trophic levels and are recycled. Balls that move toward the unsustainable side get buzzers and error lights.

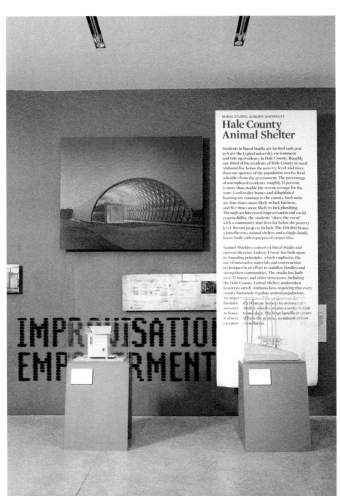

INTO THE OPEN: POSITIONING PRACTICE

by: Project Projects, saylor+sirola

for: Slought Foundation, Parsons The New
School for Design

in: New York, USA

Project Projects was commissioned to design the New York installation of the American pavilion for the 2008 Venice Architectural Biennale. The exhibition featured socially engaged and diverse architecture practices that are redefining American architecture. To emphasize their use of low-cost, high-impact solutions for creating immersive and interactive environments, the exhibition's walls and furniture were painted with green chalkboard paint. Visitors were then encouraged to write feedback and ideas anywhere they pleased. The exhibition design was created in collaboration with saylor+sirola.

THIS IS NOT A TROJAN HORSE

by: Futurefarmers
in: Abruzzo, Italy

THIS IS NOT A TROJAN HORSE is a human-powered wooden horse that traveled through the Abruzzo region of Italy for 12 days, collecting the seeds, tools, and products of the region's agricultural practices. It also facilitated discussions with local citizens about the changing rural landscape, where big-box stores, parking lots, and gas stations are quickly replacing pastures and cultivated land. Powered by two people, the horse's form begs the question: are we driving the machine or is the machine driving us? Messages written by locals on the horse's chalkboards echo the inherent fragility of the voices of the people who remain in the region—a wipe of the blackboard and the messages are gone. The horse becomes a roaming newspaper; news comes directly from the source and creates a connection of ideas and experiences between the farmers.

DIRTY WATER

by: Casanova Pendrill //
Elias Weinstock,
Alejandro Ortiz, Gil
Arevalo, Damaso Crespo

for: UNICEF USA

in: New York, USA

Looking for a low-cost solution that would create mass media exposure alarming the world about the thousands of children dying daily from a lack of clean water, Casanova Pendrill and UNICEF set up a vending machine for New Yorkers to buy filthy water for $1. Each bottle of dirty water comes with a "disease." There appears to be eigth varieties of disease to choose from: malaria, cholera, typhoid, dengue, hepatitis, dysentery, salmonella, and yellow fever. The choice was up to the buyer. Shocking the public into awareness of the problems and dangers children must face when they do not have clean water to drink, UNICEF's bottled dirty water engaged over 7,500 pedestrians and increased the number of donations beyond all expectations. Worldwide media exposure generated a large amount of text message donations. Moreover, each $1 in the vending machine supports UNICEF in providing clean water to children.

TOOLS FOR CHANGE

TOOLS FOR CHANGE

by: David Rager
for: The Ecology Center
in: San Juan Capistrano, USA

TOOLS FOR CHANGE is an exhibition and general store that promotes healthy homes and a sustainable community by connecting people, products, ideas, and resources. The exhibition challenges visitors to pledge to make simple, positive changes in their daily tasks and choices and to share their new skills and knowledge with friends and neighbors. The store sells affordable, environmentally friendly tools for following through with that pledge. David Rager's overarching branding of the exhibition and store brings the message and the action together.

THE WATERSHED

by: David Rager
for: The Ecology Center
in: San Juan Capistrano, USA

THE WATERSHED is a mobile learning unit that teaches children and adults about Southern California's watershed. Its small wooden shed unfolds to reveal learning stations that educate participants about how they can make a difference in the water cycle. David Rager created the branding for the project, which uses simple graphics for signage and integrates easily with the textures of the shed's plywood exterior. The playful graphic forms and the use of bright color appeal to kids and adults, establishing a fun atmosphere for learning and participation.

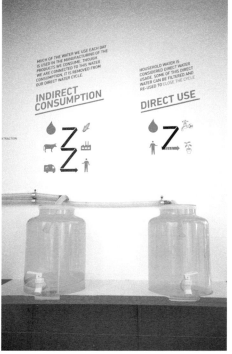

THE WATER SHED

A WATERSHED IS AN AREA WHERE WATER FROM DIFFERENT SOURCES, SUCH AS THE RAIN, STREAMS AND OUR HOMES, COME TOGETHER AND JOIN NATURE'S GREATER WATER CYCLE. HERE, IN "THE WATER SHED," WE'LL EXPLORE WHERE OUR WATER COMES FROM AND THE EVERYDAY CHOICES THAT AFFECT OUR FUTURE SUPPLY, AND THE FUTURE HEALTH OF OUR COMMUNITY.

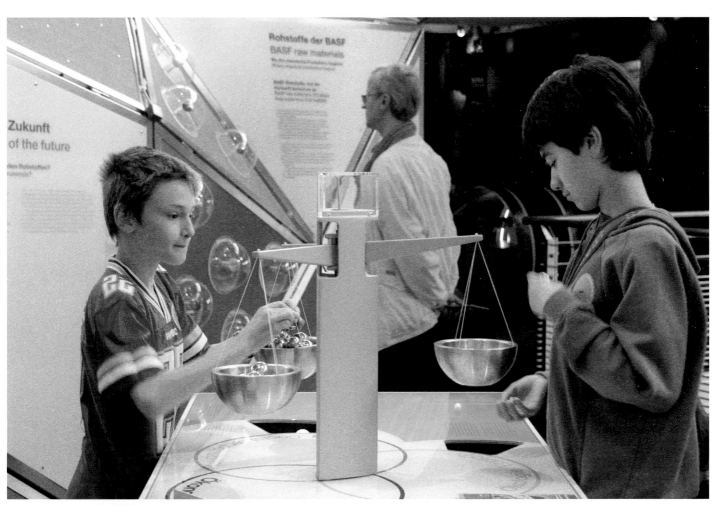

SUSTAINABILITY BALANCE

by: flying saucer
for: BASF
in: Ludwigshafen, Germany

Created for the BASF visitor center in Ludwigshafen, Germany, the SUSTAINABILITY BALANCE is an interactive exhibit that explains the modern interpretation of sustainability. Built as a scale with three parts, it demonstrates the effort required to achieve the perfect equilibrium of economic growth, environmental protection, and social responsibility. By transferring the theoretical meaning of sustainability into an experiential physical representation, the exhibit leaves visitors with a better understanding of what needs to be done to achieve sustainability.

SPIRITS OF THE FOREST

by: a secret club
in: Aarhus, Denmark

SPIRITS OF THE FOREST was an interactive story about social responsibility that introduced the environment to kids as a world of magical spirits. It was lead by the creative team at a secret club, who believe in collaborative play as part of the learning experience. SPIRITS OF THE FOREST had three parts: a meeting in the forest, where kids dressed up as spirits and picked up trash; an animated film screening about spirits; and a studio project that encouraged them to draw spirits of their own.

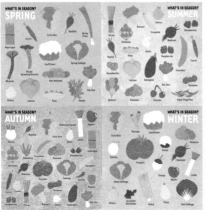

E.G. ECO GUIDE — ST. JOHN'S SCHOOL LEADING BY EXAMPLE

by: Studio Baum //
      Sam Baum, Jessica Baum
for: Creative Partnerships
in: Epping, U.K.

Studio Baum helped direct an 18-month education project with St. John's School in Epping, England. The school's rural surrounding was used to explore environmental issues. Artwork, recipes made with seasonal and local produce, and a report on the school's energy consumption were all produced by students and compiled as a book at the end of the project. Studio Baum helped run workshops to guide the content creation of the book, which served as an inspiration to other schools for educating students on the environment using simple projects that are available to everyone.

TRAVELLING SHED

by: **What if: projects //**
Ulrike Steven

for: **Surrey Arts**

in: **Surrey, U.K.**

Each inhabitant of the United Kingdom consumes the resources of six hectares per year on average — the equiva-
lent of 200 by 300 meters. The average ecological footprint
is about 800 times the size of the average back garden in
the county of Surrey. Sixty thousand square meters is the
area needed to produce the resources one consumes, and
to absorb the waste. Aiming to make the alarming facts
and figures more tangible and raise the issue of sustainable
living, What if: projects set up a typical Surrey garden shed
in the shopping centers of Farnham, Esher, and Staines.
True to the motto "Don't mow it, grow it!" the **TRAVELLING
SHED** project advertises the beauty of a productive wildlife
habitat in property-development style.

VACANT LOT INSTALLATION

by: What if: projects
for: London Festival of Architecture
in: London, U.K.

Hundreds of would-be gardeners in London's inner city are on waiting lists for scarce allotment plots—and yet there is an abundance of growing space available on paved surfaces, in empty lots, and in other unconventional spaces. The VACANT LOT program created 700 new allotment plots (equaling two acres of land) from these unused spaces by building custom-made timber planters or designing special builders bags. Sheds and water storage structures were also added to many of the allotments. The program not only provides city dwellers with a means of growing fresh food, but strengthens communities as gardeners and neighbors socialize and work together.

FRUIT CITY

by: Vahakn

for: Fruit City

in: London, U.K.

In an initiative to remind city dwellers of the edible nature all around them, **FRUIT CITY** began mapping the trees and inviting others to do the same at fruitcity.co.uk. Their message engages people with the nature around them and serves as a reminder that buying apples shipped from Holland is a waste of money and resources when apples are growing nearby in North London. In addition to tree locations, **FRUIT CITY**'s website lists projects like community orchard plantings, and unusual recipes for pies, jam, and wine.

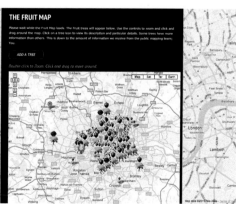

BANKSIDE BIRTHDAY BARROWS PARADE: 10TH BIRTHDAY ANNIVERSARY OF TATE MODERN

by: Studio Public, COLOCO
for: Tate Modern, Bankside Open
     Spaces Trust
in: London, U.K.

The 10th birthdays of the Tate Modern and the Bankside Open Spaces Trust were celebrated with a colourful wheelbarrow parade around the area's parks and open spaces. Customized wheelbarrows included a giant watering can, a barrow that plays rock and roll music, one that opens into a cocktail bar, and a double-decker barrow to carry more plants. A tribute to urban nature and community activity, 10 of the wheelbarrows were decorated by adults and children from the gardens they were destined to, during workshops in the months before the parade. Outweighing the high workload, the planting day proved an engaging, fun experience for over 200 local people of all ages and backgrounds.

THE IDEA OF A TREE

by: mischer'traxler

in: Vienna, Austria

A tree is a product of a specific time and place; it develops according to its surroundings and records its environment in its growth process. **THE IDEA OF A TREE** brings these recording qualities into the production process. Using solar energy to translate the intensity of the sun, a mechanical apparatus makes one object a day. The length, height, thickness, and color of the resulting object all depend on the amount of sunlight it received that day—it becomes a three-dimensional representation of the day and space where it was produced. This industrialized locality is not about local culture, craftsmanship, or resources. Instead it deals with the climatic and environmental factors surrounding the process.

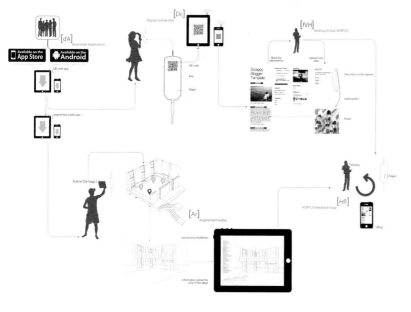

H.O.R.T.U.S AND URBAN ALGAE FARM

by: ecoLogicStudio
for: AA School of Architecture
in: London, U.K.

The exhibition **H.O.R.T.U.S.** and the **URBAN ALGAE FARM** presented new gardening prototypes that explore possible forms of urban renewable energy and agriculture in the future. Visitors were invited to interact with hanging gardens of algae by blowing into the bags, which in turn contributed to the algae's growth, and scanning a QR code on each bag, which linked them to information about the algae. The visitor's scans fed a second virtual garden that grew on a screen in the gallery. By acknowledging the role that algae could play in the future of energy production, ecoLogicStudio created a way for visitors to engage with what may be a common energy source in the future.

ESST MISFITS!

by: Culinary Misfits //
Lea Brumsack,
Tanja Krakowski
in: Berlin, Germany

A normal harvest yields a certain amount of misfits—carrots, beets, pota toes, and cucumbers that have physical imperfections. They taste the sam as the rest of the harvest, but are thrown away because supermarkets o consumers will not buy them. Once a month, Culinary Misfits takes over th market kitchen at Berlin's Markthalle Neun in Kreuzberg, where they pre pare food from vegetables that grew either too crooked, too big, or too smal By cooking these delicious vegetables from local farms, they raise aware ness of the wasted food and energy our unrealistic expectations create.

TELLER STATT TONNE

by: Slow Food, wurstsack //
Hendrik Haase
in: Berlin, Germany

TELLER STATT TONNE (Plate Instea
of Waste Bin) is a public awarenes
campaign that protests food waste
After being sorted out during harves
or picked over on store shelves, an es
timated 40 percent of food is throw
away—an amount that wastes local and global resources. Usin
aesthetically discarded foods, Slow Food Germany, the Evange
lischer Entwicklungsdienst (Church Development Service), an
Brot für die Welt (Bread for the World) prepare lunches open t
the public. The campaign's bright yellow logo, a cross between
plate and a garbage bin, playfully challenges the participant's ow
contribution to food waste while inviting them to eat lunch and b
a part of change.

YOUTH FOOD MOVEMENT

by: wurstsack //
Hendrik Haase
for: Youth Food Movement
in: Germany, Worldwide

The YOUTH FOOD MOVEMENT is a network of young people who are actively
changing the future of food and farming.
Their work realigns local and regional
food systems with the principles of justice
and sustainability. The group, which relies on volunteers to start farmer's mar-
kets, plant gardens on college campuses, and organize public protest meals
and actions, needed posters and flyers to recruit new participants. Hendrik
Haase created a fresh campaign that takes its inspiration from the handmade, grassroots spirit of the organization. It conveys the energy of the
movement by listing immediate ideas for action including buying without
barcodes, planting herbs in old shoes, and finding inspiration in foods found
in farmer's markets.

EAT-IN

by: Youth Food Movement

in: Halle (Saale), Germany

The young farmers, cooks, artisans, activists, artists, and students of the Youth Food Movement organize regular eat-ins as part of their mission. These public protest meals serve nutritious, organic, and fair food that is gathered, prepared, and shared in public spaces by the participants. The EAT-IN in Halle an der Saale, which was staged under an autobahn bridge, referenced the groups rejection of the unsustainable food supply and consumption network and emphasized its support of the ideals of their partner group, Slow Food.

ON/OFF

by: **What if: projects,
h2dance**

for: NKLA, Kent County
Council

in: U.K.

ON/OFF, a public art project by h2dance and What if: projects, was staged at a defunct auto showroom in a U.K. industrial park. It gave audience members control of the piece by harnessing their physical power to produce electricity for the pop-infused show of break dance, tap, and modern dance. Electrical power was produced by riding a set of bicycles on either side of the space—if the riding stopped, the lights went out and the music disappeared. The participatory nature of the event and the consequences of audience action or inaction created an awareness of how much energy we use—and take for granted.

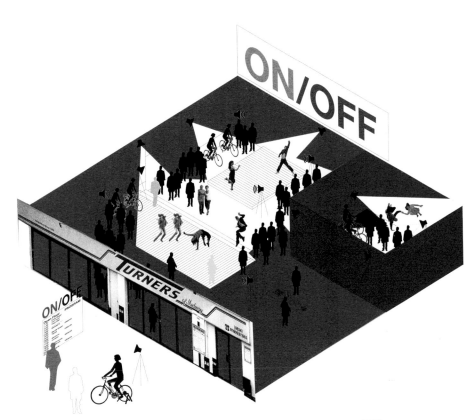

CARS INTO BICYCLES

by: Folke Köbberling,
    Martin Kaltwasser
in: Santa Monica, USA

Köbberling and Kaltwasser staged a version of their **CARS INTO BICYCLES** project in Los Angeles with students from the Art Center College of Art and Design. Over the course of three months, the group turned several parking spaces of Santa Monica's Bergamot Station into a workshop where they transformed a Saab Turbo 900 into two functional bicycles. The project promotes the idea of the potential that lies in our waste and that the world's unsustainable habits are not a lost cause—we can find innovative ways to change them and make them environmentally friendly.

DER STROMFRESSER

by: Mindpirates //
Ralf Schmerberg
for: ENTEGA
in: Hamburg, Germany

DER STROMFRESSER (The Energy Hog) is an igloo built from 322 running refrigerators, a monumental walk-in installation, set up to represent the massive amount of energy wasted by the modern appetite for electrical power. During its installation at the Gänsemarkt in Hamburg, Germany, visitors could walk inside the structure where an altar made of appliances, lights, surge protectors, and other electrical devices blinked and glowed. The piece was created for "Denkanstösse" ("Food for Thought"), an ongoing sustainability campaign co-deveoped by Mindpirates and Trigger Happy Productions on behalf of the German energy supplier ENTEGA. Accompanied by an informative magazine, the campaign takes a creative, experience-based approach to deliver messages about environmental awareness.

WORLD CLIMATE REFUGEE CAMP

by: Hermann Josef Hack

in: Berlin, Germany

By the year 2050, the United Nations estimates that 200 million people will become climate refugees. In his project **WORLD CLIMATE REFUGEE CAMP**, German artist Hermann Josef Hack uses cardboard and fabric remnants to build hundreds of miniature refugee tents, which he installs in public spaces. The tents are painted with graffiti, anti-refugee slogans, names of at-risk countries, and the name of the project. His work addresses the injustice of turning those who have contributed least to climate change into its biggest victims.

KLIMAT EKONOMI POLITIK — HUR HÄNGER DET IHOP?

by: Riksutställningar,
     Spring Street Studio //
     Hanna Werning
in: Stockholm, Sweden

KLIMAT EKONOMI POLITIK—HUR HÄN-GER DET IHOP? (free translation: Climate, Economics, Politics — How Are They Connected?) is a touring outdoor exhibition about climate, politics, and economics. A good deal of alarming information is displayed in three attractively designed exhibition "towers"; a key topic is the rapid increase in emissions of greenhouse gases during the last 50 years as a result of political decisions, imprudent behavior, and economic forces. Aimed at people who are usually not very interested in ecological matters to become curious and alarmed about climate change, Spring Street Studio's design steers clear from green clichés. Using typography, a range of pictogram-style illustrations, and virtually no photographic imagery, the exhibition distinguishes itself with a contemporary graphic look. In terms of color, too, the seemingly mandatory shades of green are avoided. Produced by Riksutställningar in collaboration with the Swedish Museum of Natural History and WWF in Stockholm, the exhibit was shown at public places in 12 cities all across Sweden. The accompanying catalog is designed as an exercise booklet and contains texts and thought-provoking work examples, and stickers about the climate changes.

MALL-TERATIONS

by: Carolina Cisneros,
Marcelo Ertorteguy,
Mateo Pinto, Sara
Valente, Hester
Street Collaborative

in: New York, USA

MALL-TERATIONS is a temporary urban intervention located on the Allen Street Pedestrians Malls on the Lower East Side in New York City. Conceived to revitalize the underutilized Allen Street corridor into a vibrant public park, **MALL-TERATIONS** celebrates the immigrant history of the neighborhood and invites its residents to actively take part in the reshaping of their environment towards a better future. As such, the sustainable approach goes beyond the use of reclaimed and recycled materials, into communicating the power and opportunities of individual and community engagement. The project is supported by the Department of Transportation of New York Urban Art Program.

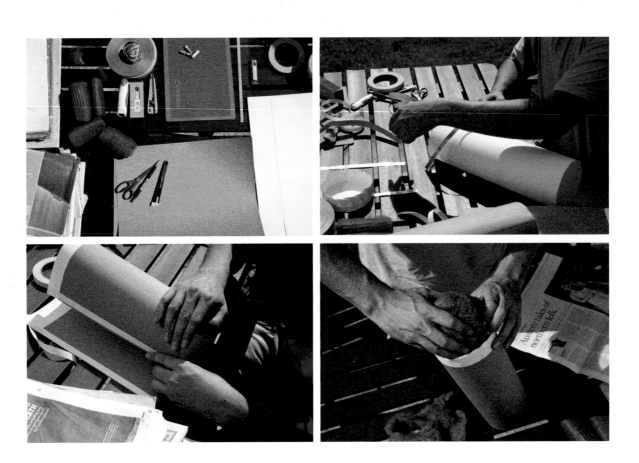

BIG BUTTS PROJECT

by: Nearly Normal Studio //
    Elias Torres, Jaime Kiss
in: London, U.K.

Elias Torres and Jaime Kiss of Nearly Normal Studio noticed that cigarette butts are thrown on streets and sidewalks every day, causing a substantial amount of litter. And no one seems to care or notice. In an effort to make people think about the trash they are throwing on the ground, they fashioned some oversized butts out of paper and steel wool and threw them in public places. A short film secretly documents the reactions of smokers and passers-by.

MANIFEST DENSITY!

by: Southern Exposure //
    Mark Reigelman, Jenny Chapman
for: The Graue Family Foundation
in: San Francisco, USA

MANIFEST DESTINY! was a temporary, site-specific installation. The rustic cabin occupied one of the last unclaimed spaces in downtown San Francisco. Using a 19th-century architectural style and vintage building materials, the structure is both an homage to the romantic spirit of the Western myth and a commentary on the arrogance of westward expansion.

INDEX

CAUSE AND EFFECT — VISUALIZING SUSTAINABILITY

Edited by Sven Ehmann, Stephan Bohle, and Robert Klanten
Preface and chapter introductions by Stephan Bohle
Project descriptions by Anna Sinofzik and Rebecca Silus for Gestalten

Layout and design by Jonas Herfurth for Gestalten
Typefaces: Nautinger by Moritz Esser, Sequencia by Matt Burvill from foundry www.gestaltenfonts.com; Newberlin by Peter Verheul
Cover design by Jonas Herfurth for Gestalten, sticker design by Hu2 Design, image "Light Switch"©iStockphoto.com/pixhook

Project management by Lucie Ulrich for Gestalten
Production management by Janine Milstrey for Gestalten
Translation by Karl Hoffmann
Proofreading by Transparent Language Solutions
Printed by Graphicom, Vicenza
Made in Europe

Published by Gestalten, Berlin 2012
ISBN 978-3-89955-443-4

Bibliographic information published by the Deutsche Nationalbibliothek.
The Deutsche Nationalbibliothek lists this publication in the Deutsche Nationalbibliografie; detailed bibliographic data are available online at dnb.d-nb.de.

None of the content in this book was published in exchange for payment by commercial parties or designers; Gestalten selected all included work based solely on its artistic merit.

This book was printed according to the internationally accepted ISO 14001 standards for environmental protection, which specify requirements for an environmental management system.

This book was printed on paper certified by the FSC®.

MIX
Paper from responsible sources
FSC® C013123

Gestalten is a climate-neutral company. We collaborate with the nonprofit carbon offset provider myclimate (www.myclimate.org) to neutralize the company's carbon footprint produced through our worldwide business activities by investing in projects that reduce CO_2 emissions (www.gestalten.com/myclimate).

myclimate
Protect our planet